Does God have a Sense of Humor?

Does God have a Sense of Humor?

Stan Pollack

To order additional copies of this book, contact:
Xlibris Corporation
1-888-795-4274
www.Xlibris.com
Orders@Xlibris.com
82452

Contents

BOOKS BY STAN POLLACK

THE GOLDEN AGE OF TONGUE KISSING

Weaves a memorable story of growing up experiences spiced with laugh-out-loud humor.

SPECIFIC INTENT

Is a fast moving detective vs. a fugitive story, placing the characters in ports of call around the world.

THE GRAVESEND CONNECTION

With a masterful grasp of what was at stake in WWII, the author effectively produces a historical novel of the time when nations of the world reluctantly descended into a tumultuous war.

DEDICATED TO MY WIFE, MARSHA

"Dear God, what a genius I was when I wrote all my books."

"Dear God, what a genius you were to have Marsha edit this one."

INTRODUCTION

DOES GOD HAVE A SENSE OF HUMOR?

WITH ALL DUE respect, the question has no answer unless we come to terms with the age-old question, IS THERE A GOD? This is no easy chore, but let's explore this in an orderly and rational fashion.

FACTS ... MYTHS ... THEORIES ... RELIGIONS

FACTS: Things that actually happened or are true and agree with reality.

MYTHS: Any imaginary people or things thought to be real.

THEORIES: Implies considerable evidence in support of a formulated general principle explaining certain phenomena.

RELIGIONS: Here is the rub! Religion is a hybrid of facts, myths and theories.

RELIGIOUS BELIEVERS

May or may not belong to an organized group. They believe there is a divine superhuman power or powers to be obeyed and worshipped. Religion involves a code of ethics, rituals and philosophy.

RELIGIOUS HEDGERS

1. FREE THINKERS: Rationalists who believe in God as a creative moving force, but otherwise reject formal religion and its doctrines of divine authority as incompatible with reason.

2. INFIDELS: Those not believing in a certain religion or a prevailing religion.

NON-RELIGIOUS BELIEVERS

1. ATHEISTS: Reject all religious beliefs and deny the existence of God.

2. AGNOSTICS: Believe the human mind cannot yet know whether there is a God.

Question: If God made the universe and Man, who made God?
Answer: In one word, Man! God did not create Man in his own image, Man created God in his own image. Man's role on this planet is not to worship God, but to create him. An honest God is the noblest work of man. God must exist for Mankind to be happy. At first, Man's fears and superstitions conceived "The Gods." Then, a more intelligent Man introduced the concept of a universal God. Because the idea of God comes from Man, each man becomes his or her own special God. The kingdom of God is within Man. The glory of God is within Man fully alive on earth, not heaven. Man is the sole maker of his life,

his rewards and his punishments. Man is the master of his fate and the captain of his soul.

Question: Can Man get whatever he needs to meet life's demands without prayer?
Answer: Yes! Man is the only living being who says, or needs to say, prayers. Man cannot expect his prayers to be answered, he must work for them. Man can get whatever he needs to meet life's demands without prayer.

Question: Is faith in the same ballpark as prayers?
Answer: Sort of! Faith is an illogical belief in the occurrence of the improbable. Faith is defined as a belief in something for which there is no evidence. Sometimes, faith is transferred from God to worldly beings such as the medical profession, stockbrokers, ponzi schemers and lawyers.

Minister in Church: I convened this faith meeting to pray for rain during the drought. My question is, "Why didn't any of you bring an umbrella?"

Man, hanging off protruding tree branch after falling off a steep cliff:
Help me, please. Is anybody up there?
Deep Voice: Yes my son. I am up here.
Man: Who is this?
Deep Voice: It's the Lord.
Man: Can you help me?
God: Certainly, my son. You must have faith and say a prayer, and I will catch you after you let go of the branch.
Man thinking, then shouts: Is there anybody else up there?

God: I noticed you standing next to a big dead dinosaur. How did a little guy like you kill it?
Little guy: I have faith in my club.
God: How big is your club?
Little guy: Well, there are about a hundred of us!

A disabled man wanders into a church on crutches. He slowly climbs a dozen stairs to reach the holy water. He splashes some on his legs and throws the crutches away. An altar boy watches all this and runs to the rectory to tell the priest.

Priest: My son, you have just witnessed a genuine miracle through an act of faith. By the way, where is the man now?

Altar boy: Laying on his fucking back at the bottom of the altar steps, moaning "Jesus Christ," but not in a good way.

THE EVOLUTION OF THE GOD GENE

Science reporter and author, Nicholas Wade, explored "the evolution of the God gene." Recent research into the history of early man is pointing to a new perspective on religion, one that seeks to explain why religious behavior has occurred in societies at every stage of development and in every religion of the world. Religion exists because it was wired into our neutral circuitry before the human population dispersed from its African homeland.

For atheists, it is not a welcome thought that religion evolved because it conferred essential benefits on early human societies and their successors. If religion is a life belt, it is difficult to portray it as useless. For believers, it may seem threatening to believe that the mind has been shaped to believe in gods, since the actual existence of the divine may then seem less likely.

However, the evolutionary perspective on religion does not necessarily threaten the central position of either side. That religious behavior was favored by natural selection neither proves or disproves the existence of gods. What evolution has done is to endow people with a genetic predisposition to learn the religion of their community just as they are predisposed to learn its language. With both religion and language it is culture, not genetics, that dictates what is learned.

Religion served the ancestral human population as an invisible government. It bound people together, committing them to put their communal needs ahead of their own needs. Because of fear of divine punishment, people followed rules of self-restraint toward members of the community. It encouraged them to give their lives in battles against outsiders. Groups fortified by religious beliefs prevailed over others lacking religion. The genes that propelled the mind toward ritual would eventually become universal.

A propensity to learn religion in one's environment became so firmly implanted in the human circuitry that religion was retained when hunter/gatherers began to settle in fixed communities 15,000 years ago. Later, in larger societies, religion became the ruler's source of authority. Roman emperors called themselves chief priests and/or living gods. Religion was even harnessed to vital tasks such as agriculture. Spring and autumn festivals helped get crops planted and harvested at the right time.

Given this background, the question arises . . . could the evolutionary perspective on religion become the basis for some kind of détente between religion and science? For example, if atheists have respect for evolution and its workings, and regard religious behavior as an evolved instinct, they may understand religion's role in human development.

Religion is often and rightly blamed for its excesses in promoting persecution and warfare. It gets less credit for patching up the moral fabric of society. The religious leaders are responsible for directing the people for good or bad purposes.

IN DEFENCE OF RELIGION

QUESTION: So, it appears as if Man should put religion onto the back burner?
ANSWER: Not necessarily. This is up to each individual. He or she can give up their godly powers to the abstract if it brings happiness and inner peace. If it works for them, why not? These are individual decisions that can be changed from time to time and must be respected. Religion is the hope and the anchor of safety from dismal fears and anxious self-devouring cares. The effectiveness of religion lies precisely in what is not rational in the unforeseen, the miraculous,

and the extraordinary. Religion without mystery ceases to be religion. Religion is not primarily a set of beliefs, a collection of prayers or a series of rituals. Religion is first and foremost a way of seeing. It can't change facts about the world we live in, but it can change the way we see those facts, and that in itself can make a difference. We need to believe the world we live in makes sense . . . there is really a pattern. Long ago people told stories of how God created the world, the sun and the moon and the first humans. That was part of the process of persuading themselves the world made sense. It was their way of assuring themselves there were reasons for everything that happened. Today, we have many of our questions answered by science. Yet, the fundamental questions continue to linger. Why is there a world? Why did humans come into being? Why do people have thoughts and memories and longings? There are no scientific answers to these questions.

And so, religion offers the recognition of God's greatness and our limitations. This is why there are no atheists in foxholes and only a few in hospitals. As long as there are algebra exams there will be prayers in schools. It is not because people are hypocrites ignoring God when things are going smoothly and suddenly discovering him when they are in trouble. The fact is there are no atheists in foxholes because times like these bring us face to face with our limitations. Those of us, who are usually so self-confident, so secure in our ability to control things, suddenly learn that some things are beyond the limits of our own power. During these moments we need to turn to a power much greater than ourselves. People have always discovered God when they are at the limits of their own strength. Yet, there are people today who barely see the limits of their own power. This leaves little room for God to enter into their lives.

Question: Now, back to the original question . . . Does God have a sense of humor?
Answer: Of all creatures on earth, Man alone possesses a sense of humor. Man has the ability to laugh at life. Laughter has much to do with inner pain. It exaggerates the anxieties and absurdities we feel. Man can gain distance and relief through laughter. We are all here

for just a short spell, so get all the good laughs you can. Religious believers should consider that God cannot be solemn or he would not have blessed Man with the gift of laughter. So, if God is in every Man, then, yes indeed, GOD HAS A SENSE OF HUMOR.

A FINAL THOUGHT

I have never understood why some believers consider it derogatory to suppose that God has a sense of humor. One possible reason may reflect the fact that there is a total absence of humor in the bible. If Man has the ability to laugh, smile or smirk, than he, without any reservations, has the right to incorporate humor into a humorless bible whenever and wherever the funny bone starts to tickle.

One of the functions of good humor is to speak the unspeakable. Nothing here is sacred . . . death, disease, disability, misfortune, tragedy, disappointment, grief, frustration, and most of all, God, Heaven or Hell. A religion that is never anything but solemn becomes most certainly never anything but mechanical. So, I proceed without embarrassment or apology to take sacred names and events in vain. DOES GOD HAVE A SENSE OF HUMOR is supported by the most famous and interesting stories from the Old and New Testaments. Believers, please be assured God will nod his approval.

CHAPTER ONE

THE BIBLE

THE BIBLE, THE best selling book of all time, is the most widely revered book of civilization. The stories of the Bible moved the minds and hearts of people for centuries before they were written down. The books of the Bible include folklore, fable, myth, history and endless fantasies about people and their lives. These legends hold the thoughts and deeds that have shaped lives through the centuries. Many of the laws and commandments laid down in the Bible are the foundation of the moral values and laws of Western civilization.

It all began with story telling long before anyone had learned to read or write. Stories about God and his people were passed along by word of mouth from generation to generation. Some stories told how God created the universe; others related the history of the Hebrew people. The narratives were carefully constructed to explain how God interacts in people's lives.

The people of the Ancient Near East had developed tales about warlike Gods and superhuman heroes. The Hebrew people, however, were unique. They recognized a single true God who held all of creation in his hand. The characters in the Hebrew sagas were very much of flesh and blood.

Although the word "Bible" means book and has been treated as a single book for much of its history, it is, in fact, many books. The Bible is a collection of the literature of Ancient Israel as well as the events and teaching of early Christianity. The Jewish Bible consists entirely of the Old Testament. The Christian Bible contains both the Old and New Testaments.

The Old Testament is a compilation of laws, history, and literary writings originally found on scrolls and written at different times. Judaism, the religion of the Jewish people, is based upon two fundamental texts . . . The Old Testament and the Talmud. The Old Testament, for the most part, covers a history of civil rights struggles by the Hebrew people against their oppressors. The Talmud consists of collected sets of writings laying out Jewish civil and religious laws, including prophesies of the Ancient Hebrews.

Jesus Christ is considered to be the inspiration for Christianity, although the word "Christian" was not used in his lifetime. The primary source of information about him in the New Testament comes from the Gospels of Matthew, Mark, Luke and John. The New Testament doesn't offer a new doctrine of God, but simply proclaims that the Old Testament God has definitively proclaimed a Messiah. The God of Abraham, Isaac, and Jacob is now the God and Father of Jesus Christ. The New Testament focuses on the death and resurrection of Jesus and his earthly ministry. These events are in a proclamation describing the hope of the Jews for a new heaven and a new earth. This consummation will be completed when Christ returns to earth. Basically, on the issue of salvation or the consequences of sin, Man can do nothing to save himself. He needs the grace of God, which can only be given through Christ.

CHAPTER TWO

CREATION

L ET'S START AT the very beginning. Already, there is a problem. There is a "slight discrepancy" as to the time frame. With the advent of "The Big Bang," the universe is more or less 13 billion years old, (who's counting), or 6,000 years old according to early biblical time tables. Since I see absolutely no humor at all in rocks and gases bouncing around the heavens for eternity, I have opted for the biblical theory in order to produce a humorous book as promised.

DAY ONE:

In the beginning God created heaven and earth. The earth was void and without form. The spirit of God was moving over the dark and deep water. And God said, "Let there be light." And there was light. And God saw that light was good. And God separated the light from the darkness. And there was evening and there was morning.

God to Angel: I've just created a 24 hour period of alternating light with darkness on earth.
Angel: What are you going to do now?

God: I think I'll call it a day.

Minister to Patient at Insane Asylum: They tell me you claim to be God. If you are the Lord I would like to ask you a question. In the Bible you say you created the universe in six days. Were those twenty four hour days or did you have a different kind of day in mind?

Patient: You'll have to forgive me; I don't like to talk shop!

DAY TWO:

And God Said, "Let there be sky in the midst of the waters and let it separate the waters from the waters." And God made the sky and separated the waters which were under the sky from the waters which were above the sky. And it was good. And God called the sky, "Heaven." And there was evening and there was morning.

Guppy #1 in fish tank: I no longer believe in God.

Guppy #2: All right. Don't believe in God. But then, tell me, who changes the water?

DAY THREE:

And God said, "Let the waters under the heavens be gathered together in one place, and let dry land appear." And it was so. God called the dry land "earth", and the water that he gathered together in one place, He called "seas". And God saw it was good. And God said, "Let the Earth put forth vegetation, plants yielding seed, and fruit trees bearing fruit in which is their seed, each according to its kind, upon the Earth." And it was so. And God saw that it was good. And there was evening and there was morning.

Minister to Farmer: Amazing what you have done with this old run down farm you purchased. Look what you and God have accomplished together.

Farmer: You're darn right. It's quite astonishing when you consider what this place looked like when God was working alone.

DAY FOUR:

And God said, "Let there be lights in the sky of the heavens to separate the day from the night, and let there be seasons and years. And, let there be lights in the sky to give light upon the earth." And, so it was. And God made two great lights – the greater light to rule the day and the lesser light to rule the night. He made stars, also. And God set the stars in the sky to give light upon the Earth. And God saw that it was good. And, there was evening and there was morning.

Shrink to elderly wife: I'm concerned about your husband. He told me when he goes to the bathroom in the middle of night, he opens the door. God then turns on the light and closes it when he's finished.
Wife: OH! No! He's been peeing in the fridge again.

Camper to friend: Look up at the sky and tell me what you see.
Friend: I see millions and millions of stars in the heavens of God.
Camper: What does it tell you?
Friend: It tells me there are millions of galaxies, and potentially, billions of planets. I observe that Saturn is in Leo. Time-wise, I deduce the time is approximately half passed three. Theologically, I can see the Lord is all-powerful and we are small and insignificant. Weather-wise, I suspect we will have a beautiful day tomorrow. What does it tell you?
Camper: Idiot! It tells me some fucking idiot stole our tent!

DAY FIVE:

And God said, "Let the waters bring forth swarms of living creatures, and let birds fly above the Earth across the sky of the heavens." So, God created the great sea monsters according to their kinds and every winged bird according to its kind. And God saw that it was good.

And God blessed them saying, "Be fruitful and multiply and fill the waters in the seas and the skies above." And, there was evening and there was morning.

A chicken and an egg were lying in bed. The chicken was smoking a cigarette with a smug smile on her face. The egg was frowning, looking very frustrated.

The Egg mutters: Well, I guess we answered that question!

DAY SIX:

And God said, "Let the earth bring forth living creatures according to their kinds." And it was so. And God made the beasts of the Earth according to their kinds, and the cattle according to their kinds, and everything that creeps upon the ground according to their kind. And, God saw that it was good.

Then God said, "Let us create Man in our image, after our likeness and let him have domination over the fish of the seas, over the birds of the air, over the cattle, over all the Earth, and over every creeping thing that creeps upon the Earth."

So, God created Man in his own image – male and female. He created them and God blessed them, and God said to them, "Be fruitful and multiply and fill the Earth and subdue it. And, have domination over the fish of the sea and over the birds of the air and over every living thing that moves upon the Earth. Behold, I have given you every plant yielding seed on the earth, and every tree with seed in its fruit. You shall have them for food, and so will every beast, every bird, everything that creeps, and everything that has the breath of life within it." And, so it was so. And there was evening and there was morning. Thus, the Heavens and the Earth were finished.

God to Angel on the 6th day: I'm also going to create a land called Israel. There will be large mountains topped with snow, fresh water lakes, trees of all kinds, sandy beaches with an abundance of sea life and soil so fertile any living plant, fruit or vegetable, can thrive upon it.

Angel: But, Lord, don't you think you are being too generous to the Israelites?

God: Not really. Just wait and see the neighbors I'm going to give them.

DAY SEVEN:

God only took six days to complete his work. However, that was in the days before unions, permits and environmental surveys. On the seventh day God rested from all he had accomplished. So, God blessed the day and hallowed it.

CHAPTER THREE

ADAM AND EVE

ALTHOUGH HE WAS the last comer among the creatures, the world was made for Man. This was God's design. Man was to find all things ready for him. God was the host that set the table and led his guest to his seat. The superiority of Man to other creatures is apparent in the very manner of his creation. Man alone, was created by the hand of God. All other living things sprang from the word of God. God molded Adam from the dust of the ground and breathed into him divine breath to become a living being. The care God exercised when fashioning every detail of the body of Man is no less important to his creation of the human soul.

God made Adam fall into a deep sleep so he could remove one of his ribs and fashion a Woman. God presented Woman to Adam and enabled them to develop the human race. Adam named her Eve, "the mother of all living things." The story of Adam and Eve stresses the unity of the sexes and their mutual complementary needs within the social structure of marriage.

THE GARDEN OF EDEN

The Garden of Eden was a garden of trees and lush vegetation planted by God and occupied by Adam and Eve. In its center stood The Tree of Life and Knowledge. The garden was not simply a luxurious paradise, but a place for human beings to live, eat, and work.

FALL FROM GRACE AND PUNISHMENT

The "Fall," refers to the disobedience and expulsion of Adam and Eve from The Garden of Eden. Initially, they enjoyed a life of ease and intimacy with God. Yet, their desire to become "Like Gods," led them to disobey God's prohibition against eating the fruit from the Tree of Knowledge.

Among the animals in the garden, the serpent was the most notable. Like Man, he stood upright on two feet and he was as tall as a camel. His superior mental gifts caused him to become an infidel. This explains his envy of Man, causing him to devise ways of bringing about Adam's death. He felt Adam would not disobey God's rules for acceptable behavior in the Garden. Thus, he approached Eve, believing the character of a woman made her more easily charmed. He lured her to the forbidden tree and bit into the forbidden fruit to prove he wouldn't die. Eve bit into the forbidden fruit and when she survived she prevailed upon Adam to share her enjoyment.

God did not question the serpent. He immediately meted out his punishment. The serpent was relegated to crawling on his belly. The serpent no longer ate the same food as man; he survived on the tiny creatures found in the earth's dust.

God then turned his attention to punishing Adam and Eve. They were banished from the Garden of Eden and condemned to a life of suffering. Adam was destined to toil his lifetime as a farmer. Eve, representing woman, was destined to suffer pain when child bearing. The couple left the Garden of Eden with their heads hanging low and settled in a barren area east of Paradise.

God to Adam: You will have a wife who will be the best of all companions. She will be beautiful, intelligent, and good natured. She will cook for you, clean for you, and take care of your every need without complaint. She will service you for life giving you undiluted physical pleasure.

Adam: Sounds good. What do I have to do to get her?

God: You must give up an arm, a leg, a rib and your right testicle.

Adam (thinking): And what do I get for just a rib?

God: Eve!

God to Eve: You will serve your husband and he shall be your master and rule over you!

Eve: Right! Got it!

GARDEN OF EDEN CHAT ROOM

ADAM: Hey! I wear the "plants" in the family!

ADAM: Stand back, Eve. I don't know how big this thing gets!

ADAM: After I take a bite out of the apple, I'm going to do what to you?

ADAM: Am I the first?
EVE: Why does everyone ask me that question?

EVE: Adam, you're home late again. Have you been unfaithful to me?
ADAM: With Whom?

THE ADAMS VERSUS THE EVES

The difference between Eves at ages 8, 18, 28, 38, 48, 58, and 68;

AT 8: You take Eve to bed and tell her a story.

AT 18: You tell Eve a story and take her to bed.

AT 28: You don't need to tell Eve a story to take her to bed.

AT 38: Eve tells you a story and takes you to bed.

AT 48: Eve tells you a story to avoid going to bed.

AT 58: You stay in bed to avoid her story.

AT 68: If you take Eve to bed, that will be a story.

HOW ADAM INTERPRETS EVE'S PERSONAL ADS

EVE SAYS	ADAM THINKS
40-ish	49
adventurous	slept with everyone
athletic	no boobs
average looking	m0000!
beautiful	pathological liar
emotionally secure	on medication
fun	annoying
gentle	dull
feminist	fat
voluptuous	very fat
large frame	pig
friendship first	former slut
open-minded	desperate
jovial	sloppy drunk
poet	depressed
romantic	frigid
professional	bitch
free spirit	junkie
wants soul mate	stalker
widow	murderer

EVE THE FIRST JEWISH MOTHER

The advent of jokes about Jewish mothers in the 20th century in America came about because men were somewhat financially successful and the extended family no longer existed. Someone had to care for the home and hearth and rear the children. Jewish mothers gradually become removed from the job markets. In reality, they were budget experts, seamstresses, short order cooks, chefs, doctor's assistants, nurses, decorators and designers. The Joke: They began living their dream lives vicariously through the lives of their children. This in turn led to more jokes about their children's neuroses and problems, serving as targets for scoffing the Jewish mother.

The Dictionary defines Jewish mothers as: Jewish Mother (n) slang. 1) A martyr, creator of guilt, person impossible to please.

Jewish mother to whomever: It's okay. Go ahead and enjoy yourself. Don't worry. I'll be just fine. I don't mind staying home alone, being lonely. I like to sit in the dark. I'll be just fine. It's nothing at all. It will go away.

Jewish mother to whomever: Don't ask what kind of a day I had. It was the kind of a day when a call from you would have made all the difference in the world.

Jewish mother to whomever: Don't worry that I'm not eating so good. I just don't want to be stuck with a mouthful if you should call.

Jewish mother to whomever: How much longer will I be around to bother you?

Jewish mothers' concerns are different for her sons and daughters. It's education at any cost for the son. It's a quality marriage to a doctor or a lawyer for the daughter.

Catholic mother #1: My son is a priest. When he walks into a room everyone calls him, "Father."

Catholic mother #2: My son is a bishop. When he walks into a room everyone calls him, "Your Grace."

Catholic mother #3: My son is a cardinal. When he walks into a room everyone calls him, "Your Eminence."

Jewish mother: My son is six feet three inches tall. He is single just like your sons. He is drop dead handsome and carries a wide smile all the time. He has broad shoulders and dresses like a model. I have to add that as far as money is concerned, he is loaded. He has a muscular body as well as a tight ass. When he walks into a room, women gasp, "Oh My God!"

GRANDMOTHERS ARE JEWISH MOTHERS TOO

A little boy and his Jewish grandmother were walking along the beach when a huge wave appeared out of nowhere and swept the child out to sea.

Grandmother: Oh! God! Please return my beloved grandson to me. Please, I beg you. Send him back safely.

Another big wave washed in and deposited the little boy on the beach at the grandmother's feet. She picked him up, looked him over and looked up towards the heavens.

Grandmother to God: He had a hat!

JEWISH MOTHER AND HER HUSBAND

Italian wife: Gino, you're the world's best lover!

French wife: Jacques, you are marvelous in bed!

Jewish wife: Oy, Jake! The ceiling needs painting.

Italian husband: I rubbed my wife all over with olive oil and we made love. She screamed for five minutes.

French husband: I rubbed my wife all over with sweet butter and we made love. She screamed for half an hour.

Jewish husband: I rubbed my wife all over with chicken fat and we made love. She screamed for six hours.

Italian and French husbands in unison: Six hours, six hours. How did you make her scream for six hours?

Jewish husband: I wiped my hands on the curtains.

THE JEWISH PRINCESS – JEWISH MOTHER IN TRAINING

The Jewish princess took her boyfriend home to meet her parents.

Mother to boyfriend: So, what do you do for a living?

Boyfriend: I own some property.

Princess: Some property. He owns a chain of malls.

Mother: And where do you live?

Boyfriend: I've got an apartment in town.

Princess: An apartment! He has a 10,000 square foot penthouse.

Mother: And what are your prospects?

Boyfriend: I'm looking to expand.

Princess: Expand! He's planning to buy Bloomingdales!

Just then the boyfriend sneezes.

Mother: Do you have a cold?

Princess: A cold. He's got double pneumonia!

Princess, at front door with boyfriend: You want me to give you a quickie here. Are you crazy?

Boyfriend: Don't worry. It will only take 30 seconds at the most.

Princess: Jewish girls don't do that.

Boyfriend: Oh, come on! Just 20 seconds. That's my best time.

Jewish mother, opening the door: Honey, either give him a quickie or tell him to get lost. Either way, daddy wants him to stop leaning on the intercom.

CHAPTER FOUR

CAIN AND ABEL

WICKEDNESS CAME INTO the world with the first being born of a woman. His name was Cain, the oldest son of Adam and Eve. Here lies the curious story of Cain and his younger brother, Abel.

Cain, a farmer, offered a sacrifice to the Lord of grain, while Abel, a shepherd, offered a sacrifice from his flock. Abel selected the best from among his animals, but Cain ate his meal first and offered God a few left over grains of seed. God did not receive Cain's offering with favor. Yet, Cain thought he had been wronged. He believed God ruled the world with arbitrary power. Abel maintained God rewarded discretionary good deeds.

The brothers argued in the fields. Abel, fearing for his life, warned Cain that God would avenge Abel should Cain slay him. This added to Cain's anger and he attacked his brother. Abel was stronger and Cain would have gotten the worst of it. Abel got the upper hand and Cain begged for mercy. The gentle Abel released his hold. This gave a free Cain the opportunity to re-attack his brother. As Abel fell to the ground, Cain pelted him with stones. One struck Abel on the neck and inflicted death.

After committing the murder, Cain decided to flee. God stopped him in his tracks and questioned him. "Where is Abel, thy brother?"

Cain answered, "Am I my brother's keeper?"

Cain refused to confess his guilt. He insisted he had never seen a man killed, and how was he supposed to know stones would take a life.

The Lord banished Cain to wander the earth. Cain was fearful wild animals would devour him to avenge Abel. God inscribed the letter, "O", his holy name, upon Cain's forehead to protect him from a possible onslaught of beasts. He told the animals that Cain was protected. While Cain had shed blood, there was nobody to tell him what actions might cause death. This was the first murder ever committed. God ruled that in the future one who slays another shall himself be slain. Thus, the rule of an eye for an eye came into being. To further mark Cain as a sinner, God afflicted him with leprosy. Abel became the first martyr to die for his faith.

Prosecutor: Did you intentionally kill the victim?
Defendant: No, I did not.
Prosecutor: Do you know the penalties for perjury?
Defendant: Yes, I do. They're a hell of a lot better than the penalties for murder.

CHAPTER FIVE

NOAH

THERE WERE TEN generations between Adam and Eve and the birth of Noah. The depravity of mankind began to show itself during this period. It was a time when the sinfulness of man included idol worship. God had been patient with almost all sins except immoral lifestyles. The punishment was to cleanse and purify the earth. God created a flood for forty days and forty nights completely destroying life on the earth.

Among the peoples of the times was a man named Noah. He taught truth, knowledge, and fear of God to a hostile audience. Noah found favor with the Lord as an exemplary righteous person. As such, God selected Noah and his immediate family to remain on earth after the flood.

God instructed Noah to build a giant ark of gopher wood, which would float. The ark was completed according to God's instructions. The vessel contained a wide entrance on one side. The inside was triple decked.

Noah's next task was to gather God's chosen animals, male and female of each species to repopulate the earth after the flood. Noah and his family lived on the ark for one year waiting for the lands to dry even though it only rained for forty days. Noah released a dove, daily, to investigate conditions outside the ark. Finally, one day the dove returned to the ark with an olive branch, demonstrating the water had sufficiently retreated. It was time to leave the ark that was parked on top of Mount Ararat.

When Noah and his family stepped out of the ark onto dry land they witnessed the enormous ravages brought by the flood. God made an agreement with Noah. He promised never to send a flood of this proportion again. As proof of his promise, a rainbow appeared clear across the sky.

UNNAMED WOMEN OF THE BIBLE

Noah's wife is mentioned five times in the book of Genesis, but only in the context of being one of a group who is present. This is surprising considering how talented and efficient she must have been to have been suddenly uprooted from her home and asked to set up housekeeping in an ark filled with birds, snakes, insects and full grown animals of every species. The woman who kept everything in order in the ark for twelve months is known to us today, not by her own name, but only as, "Noah's wife."

God: Noah?

Noah: Now what?

God: You've got to take one of those hippos out of the ark and bring in another.

Noah: What for?

God: Because you have two males down there and you need to exchange one for a female.

Noah: I'm sick of all of this. I'm not bringing animals in and out. You change them if you want.

God: Come on, Noah. You know I don't work like that.

Noah: I've had enough of this stuff. I've been working my ass off for months. I'm sick and tired, I tell you.

God: Noah?
Noah: Yeah?
God: How long can you tread water?

Noah's wife to Noah: Don't let the elephants watch the rabbits.

The Bible reports Noah was 600 years old when the flood came. He
lived 350 more years after the flood, dying at the ripe old age of
950 years. An incredible feat without Medicare.

Noah: Oh, God. All this water makes me want to pee, but I can't.
God: How old are you Noah?
Noah: Over 600 years, My Lord.
God: Stop worrying! You've peed enough!

Noah: Doc, they say I'm as old as they come. Is that true?
Doctor: According to my examination, I'm alone in this room.

UNRECORDED BIBLICAL CONVERSATIONS

Upon leaving the ark, Noah was greeted by two high-powered
salesmen, who surprisingly survived the flood.
Real estate agent: Noah, I have an abundance of undeveloped land. I
can give you a good deal on a lot to build a new home.
Noah: You've got to be kidding. At my age I don't even buy green
bananas.
Agent: Have you lived in these parts all of your life?
Noah: I don't know. I haven't died yet.
Agent: Well, think it over. Talk to Noah's wife. I can offer you a 500
year fixed mortgage with prepayment privileges after the first
hundred years.

After waiting his turn, an aggressive life insurance agent approached
Noah.

Agent: Don't worry, Noah. I'm not here to sell you flood insurance. I'm here to sell you life insurance. I'll explain.

Noah (after listening carefully): I understand fully. I pay you money, and after I die you pay me money.

Agent: Exactly.

Noah: Listen, big boy, I wasn't born yesterday.

Agent: The money is for Noah's wife. It's not for you.

Noah: Then let Noah's wife buy your insurance.

Agent: By the way, Noah, how have you managed to stay married for hundreds and hundreds of years?

Noah: You just close your eyes and pretend it's not happening.

Agent: Don't let me pressure you about life insurance. Let me know tomorrow if you get up. By the way, how have you managed to live so long?

Noah: It's easy. The secret is never to argue with anyone.

Agent: That's insane! It has to be something else. Just not arguing won't keep you alive for hundreds and hundreds of years.

Noah (thinking): You know, maybe you're right!

Agent: Before you speak to Noah's wife, you should know I also offer fire insurance.

Noah: Under the terms of the policy, how much will I get if the ark burns down tomorrow?

Agent: 150 years.

Noah: Let me advise you, sir. Do you know you can't sell insurance without a license?

Agent: I knew I wasn't selling any, but I never knew the reason.

NOAH, THE WINO

Noah lost his "piousness" in his vineyard. His attempt to produce wine also produced the first person to drink to excess, the first person to utter continuous curses upon his workers, and the first person to introduce slavery.

His vineyard came about in a strange way. Noah located a grape tree that grew from a vine Adam had taken out of the Garden of Eden when he was driven out with Eve. He tasted the grapes, which had survived the flood and found them still palatable. He decided to plant and care for a cutting. A large vineyard grew from this incident.

Question: How do you make Manishewitz wine?
Answer: Squeeze his balls.

Girl on a date bluffing faultless taste and ultimate refinement, whispers to a boy: Oh, Yes! Let's have sherry-wine rather than brandy-wine. Sherry-wine is absolutely divine. When I sip it I am transported from the every day scene. The flavor, the aroma, a hilly field bathed in soft sunshine, a small brook rambling through the woods, the drowsy sounds of insects, the gentle blowing winds, all brings to mind a kind of a warmth, peace and serenity. BRANDY WINE, ON DER UTTER HAND, MAKES ME FART.

He took her to the finest restaurant on their first date.
Girl: I'm thinking of caviar to start, and then lobster with a side dish of pheasant, and that 1929 bottle of wine on the wine list. Chocolate Mousse may come later, or perhaps a flambé of some sort.
Boy: Does your mother feed you like this with 80 year old wines?
Girl: No. But, my mother doesn't want to take me home later and fuck my brains out.

Guy at bar: Hi. I couldn't help but notice the book you are reading.
Girl: It's about finding sexual satisfaction. It's quite interesting. Did you know that statistically American Indians and Polish men are the best lovers? By the way, my name is Jill. What's yours?
Guy: Flying Cloud Kowarski. Nice to meet you.

Guy at bar: I had sex with my wife before we were married. What about you?
Bartender: I don't know. What was her maiden name?

Guy: I'm dying to get laid in the worst way.
Bartender: The worst way I know is standing up in a hammock.

THE ART OF NOT PAYING FOR DRINKS

Patron: I'll have four double shots of the thirty year old whiskey and line them up on the bar.
Bartender: Wow! You just downed them as quickly as I've ever seen anyone drink. You seem to be in a hurry.
Patron: You would be too if you had what I have.
Bartender: What do you have?
Patron: Fifty cents.

Patron: I'd like to buy that old douche bag at the other end of the bar a drink.
Bartender: Sir, I don't appreciate calling my female customers "douche bags."
Patron: Sorry. You're right. That's uncalled for. Please allow me to buy that woman a cocktail.
Bartender: Madame, the gentleman at the other end of the bar would like to buy you a drink. What would you like?
Woman: How nice! I'll have a vinegar and water.

LEAVING THE BAR

Improbable happening: So, these two Irishmen walked out of a bar.

Drunk staggers out of a bar with car key in hand: They stole my car.
Cop: Where did you last see it?
Drunk: At the end of this here key.
Cop: Are you aware that your penis is hanging out of your trousers?
Drunk: Holy Shit! They got my girlfriend too.

Old man at bar to young girl: Where have you been all my life?
Young girl: Teething.

Hooker at bar: I can see you're interested in me. I'll do anything you want for $100 with one condition.

Patron: What's that?

Hooker: You have to tell me in three words.

Patron, thinking: Paint my house.

Girl, gossiping at the bar: I'm not saying that Susie's fiancé is cheap, but every time I get close to her engagement ring, I have an overwhelming desire for Cracker Jacks.

Husband to wife at a bar: My dear. I noticed you've been watching that man for some time. Do you know him?

Wife: Yes, he's my ex-husband, and he's been drinking like that since I left him, ten years ago.

Husband: Remarkable. I wouldn't have thought anyone could celebrate that long.

Menacing drunk at a bar: All you guys on this side of the room are cock suckers. Anyone got a problem with that? All the others on the other side are mother fuckers. Anyone got a problem with that?

Customer in the silent bar: Excuse me.

Drunk: You got a problem, buddy?

Customer: No, sir. I'm just on the wrong side of the room.

DESCENDANTS OF NOAH

Noah's sons, Shem, Ham and Japheth provided the roots from which humankind would spring. They became rulers over millions of people living in the area. A man named Abraham, descending from the line of Shem, was a prisoner under his rule. Abraham managed to escape his captors, becoming the father of the Hebrew peoples.

Boasting man: My family records go back to the 10th century.

Jewish friend: Mine were lost in the flood.

NOAH'S FINAL WORDS

I started out with nothing, and I still have most of it. It's hard to make a comeback when you haven't been anywhere. These days I spend a lot of time thinking about God and the hereafter. I go somewhere to get something and then wonder what I'm here after. Funny, I don't remember being absent minded. Funny, I don't remember being absent minded.

CHAPTER SIX

TOWER OF BABEL

AFTER THE FLOOD, with the spread of mankind, corruption increased again. In Babylonia hundreds of thousands of people were subject to the rule of harsh leaders who encouraged idol worship. There was a plan to build a great city and a tall tower to reach the heavens. They named the tower "Babel," meaning "Gate of God."

But, in reality, the idea was a rebellion against God. Once the tower was built they planned to wage war against God with bows and arrows. The tower reached so great a height it took a year to climb to the top. During the construction period a brick was more precious than a human being. If a worker fell and met his death no one took notice of it. If a brick dropped it would take a year to replace it. Workers and warriors began to shoot arrows towards heaven from the incomplete tower to test distances. They imagined the arrows were returning covered with blood.

God was now ready to put an end to this. He ordered the angels encompassing his throne to return to earth and muddle their languages. Thus, they could not understand one another's speech. As a result, no one knew what the other was saying. If one would ask for mortar, the other would hand him a brick. He would throw the brick at his partner in a rage and kill him. God, in this way, set one against the other and the tower remained unfinished. Shortly thereafter, the lower part sank slowly into the ground and the rest was consumed by fire. The future Hebrews in the Bible, referred to the meaning of Babel as "to confuse, mix."

The sinful builders of the tower were treated leniently by God, for He had set a high priority upon peace and harmony. He gave these people the opportunity to dwell amicably together in the future. New languages scattered the people and helped each group form tight knit societies, as birds of a feather who fly together.

SPEAKING OF LANGUAGE

Man's ability to use language makes him the dominant species on the planet. There is one other thing that separates us from the animals . . . we aren't afraid of vacuum cleaners!

Spaniard: Is there an English equivalent of Mañana?
Englishman: Yes, but it doesn't convey the name sense of urgency.

Iranian to a friend in California: Don't speak Farsi to me. We're in America. Speak Spanish.

Instructor: First, you hold the handle with one hand. Then, you dial the telephone with the other hand.
Italian immigrant: Then, what hand will I talk with?

An American, Russian, Iraqi, and an Israeli approached by a public opinion poll taker are asked to give their opinions about a current meat shortage
Poll taker: Excuse me, can you answer a few question?
American: What's "a shortage?"
Russian: What's "meat?"
Iraqi: What's "public opinion?"

Israeli: What's "excuse me?"

Teacher to teenage girl student: There are two words I'd like you to drop from your vocabulary. One is "gross," and the other is "awesome."
Student: Okay. What are they?

Teacher: Class, it's an interesting linguistic fact that in English, a double negative forms a positive. In some languages, such as Russian, a double negative is still a negative. However, there is no language in which a double positive can form a negative.
Student: Yeah! Right!

Son: Dad, what is the difference between *potentially* and *realistically?*
Father: Go ask your mother if she would sleep with Robert Redford for a million dollars. Then, ask your sister if she would sleep with Brad Pitt for a million dollars. Then, ask your brother if he would sleep with Tom Cruise for a million dollars.
Son: Okay. I asked, and they all said yes. I think I get it. POTENTIALLY, we're sitting on 3 million bucks. REALISTICALLY, we're living with two sluts and a fag.

Friend one: See those guys wearing long black coats with sidelocks. What are they?
Friend two: Chassidim.
Friend one: I see them, but what are they?

Friend one, carrying a watermelon: It's been awhile, so how have you been?
Friend two, wildly swinging his hands up and down: Don't ask, don't ask. What about you?
Friend one: Do you really want me to drop my watermelon?

CHAPTER SEVEN

SODOM AND GOMORRAH

THE TEN GENERATIONS that passed after Noah were referred to as the "Wicked Generations." These descendants were sinking from depravity to even lower and lower depths of wickedness. Evil men and idol worship led the population astray.

Wars were waged between neighboring cities and towns. Captives were taken and sold into slavery. The cities of Sodom and Gomorrah were legendary for their incorrigible wickedness. Promiscuity as a way of life found acceptance here. Nearly all the women engaged in prostitution at one time or another. Homosexuality was openly flaunted. The people treated each other in a heartless manner.

All this provoked God's wrath. The Lord was intent upon changing the ways of man. The fate of Sodom and Gomorrah served as chilling examples to other communities full of human greed and oppression. These two cities were to be examples of extreme bad behavior forever, justly deserving complete destruction in a cataclysm of brimstone and fire. The sinful inhabitants lost their own lives and their share of the future.

Thus, it was timely, that the "friend of God," a righteous man named Abraham, should make his appearance on Earth. Abraham pleaded with God to reprieve the cities if ten good men could be found to redeem the cities. God was willing to negotiate, but they could not find ten good people.

God spared Abraham's nephew, Lot, and his family. God's angel, helping them flee, warned them not to look back as Sodom was being destroyed. Lot's wife, another unnamed woman of the bible, disobeyed the command. She was destroyed as she looked back at the burning city. Her body turned into a pillar of salt.

I am glad "gay" jokes are out of the closet. They are too rich a source of humor to be kept in limited circulation.

Patient, attracted to his doctor: Doc, I have a terrible pain in my rectum.

Doctor: Okay. Let's take a look. OH! Dear God! Do you realize you have a dozen American beauty roses up there?

Patient: Never mind the roses. Just read the card!

Gay driver, with a friend, hits a truck: Oh, My! Oh, My!

Burly truck driver: You stupid son of a bitch, you drive like my grandmother, and further more, you can kiss my ass.

Gay driver, to friend: Thank God, he wants to settle out of court.

Gay, at a seedy truck stop, with a parakeet on his shoulder: Whichever one of you big bruisers can guess the weight of my parakeet can go home with me.

Truck driver: 500 pounds!

Gay guy: We've got a winner. We've got a winner!

Straight friend to Gay: If you found out they were going to drop an A-bomb on us, what would be the first thing you would do?

Gay Guy: I would screw the first thing that moved! What would you do?

Friend: Stand very still.

A salesman knocks on a door. A ten year old boy opens the door. He is wearing lipstick, hanging earrings with a cigar in one hand and a martini glass in the other.

Salesman: Excuse me, young man. Are your parents home?

Boy, puffing smoke rings: What do you fuckin' think?

Two gays went to a Ferris Wheel. One chose to ride, the other not. The wheel went around several times, dislodged and crashed to the ground. The rider landed in front of his friend.

Friend: Oh, God! Are you hurt?

Rider: Terribly hurt. Terribly hurt! Three times I went round and round, and you didn't wave once.

Guy at bar to attractive woman: Say, could I buy you a drink?

Woman: Forget it buddy. I'm a lesbian. See that young girl over there?

Guy: The blonde waitress?

Woman: Exactly! I'd like to take her home to my bed. Strip off all her clothing, nibble on her tits and lick every curve and suck every inch of that sweet young thing all night long.

Guy, bursting into tears: Oh, God!

Woman: What the hell are you crying about?

Guy: I think I'm a lesbian, too.

CHAPTER EIGHT

ARCHEOLOGY AND THE BIBLE

STUDYING THE REMAINS of evacuated ancient civilizations has played a major role in confirming the possibility that Biblical stories had actually taken place. The first meaningful attempt to identify a site of a biblical city did not occur until the mid 1880's. Surveys since, have uncovered hundreds, if not thousands, of sites. Most ancient cities have left remains behind in stratified mounds called, "Tells." Enormous quantities of broken pottery are the most common objects recovered.

Most of the ancient cities were quite small. Most had walls to protect the people from wandering robbers or enemies who wanted to conquer them. As a result of these frequent battles, cities were often conquered, destroyed and later rebuilt on the same location. The rubble and stones from a previous city were used to build the new city. Archaeologists can sometimes identify as many as ten cities erected at one location by comparing the pottery or tools or old coins found in one layer with those in layers above or below, or even with layers found in other tells. Archaeologists can estimate how many hundreds of years a particular layer represents and how people lived at that time. Thus, Archaeology expands our knowledge and comprehension of Biblical times with each new discovery.

Archeologist addressing audience: We have discovered five symbols carved on the wall of a new found cave – a woman, a donkey, a shovel, a fish, and a Star of David. We can tell certain things about these ancient people from these five carvings. Women were held in high esteem. Donkeys were trained to toil the soil. A shovel proved they used tools. They also fished as well as farmed. Finally, the Star of David indicated they were Hebrews and holy men.

Man in audience: Bullshit! Hebrew is read from right to left. This is what the carvings say. Holy Mackerel dig the ass on that woman.

CHAPTER NINE

ABRAHAM

HISTORY WAS BORN in the fertile lands from Egypt through Syria to Mesopotamia. For more than the past hundred years the picks of archeologists have been uncovering carvings, inscriptions and artifacts from the ruins in these areas. This now makes it possible to reconstruct, sometimes in amazing detail, the environment that produced the existence of Abraham. We now know far more about the age of Abraham than anyone has ever known.

Abraham lived in the early 18th century, BC, in the walled town of Ur, located in the valley of Mesopotamia, now Turkey. He lived as long before Christ's coming as we have lived after it. Ur was ruled by elderly priests when Abraham was young. The place was a bustling prosperous commercial center, somewhat past its prime.

Imagine a world saturated with ignorance and hatred, lonely and brutish, and without any hope for redemption. Now, imagine being Abraham. He hears God speaking to the first human being since Noah. God commands him, "Leave behind the life you know and I will bless the entire world through you." The Lord's call was a complete surprise. How God would accomplish his goals escaped

Abraham, and yet, with unquestionable obedience he sets out with his wife, Sarah. In time, Abraham will become the patriarch of three monotheistic faiths, Judaism, Christianity, and Islam.

God promised Abraham and his descendents possession of the land, the faith to believe in his presence, and the establishment of a new nation. Fulfillment depended upon Abraham having an heir. His wife, Sarah, was barren. She told her husband to sleep with her Egyptian maid, Hagar. Abraham meekly acceded to her suggestion and Hagar conceived immediately.

Instantly, there was a conflict between the women. Abraham abdicated his authority and permitted Sarah to abuse the pregnant Hagar. In due time, a son, named Ishmael, was born. God told Abraham that Ishmael was not his heir. Hagar and her son fled into the wilderness and made a new life for themselves.

Eventually, Ishmael married an Egyptian woman and had twelve children with her. He became the original ancestor of the people living mostly as nomads in desert areas, called the Ishmaelites. To this day, all Arabs claim to be descendants of Ishmael.

THE ARABS

FROM CAMELS TO JET TRAVEL

Arab #1, on an airplane: Call over that little Jewish old man and tell him we want two cups of coffee.

Arab #2: Hey, You! Go sit in the back of the plane, but first bring us two cups of coffee.

Old Jewish Man: Here you are. Was that quick enough?

Arab #1, taunting: Tell us, what do you think of the shape of the world?

Man: It's in terrible shape. In India, Sikhs are killing Muslims. In Africa, whites are killing blacks. In Ireland, Protestants are killing Catholics, and on airplanes, Jews are pissing in Arabs' coffee cups.

Arab traveler at Tel Aviv Airport to a stranger: Look, sir, my plane is leaving in five minutes and I need five cents for my one way ticket to get home.

Stranger: Here's a quarter. Take four more with you.

Israeli, flying on Saudi Arabian Airlines, (a fairytale): Hey, miss! Do they feed us on this airline?

Hostess: Would you like a dinner?

Israeli: What are my choices?

Hostess: Yes or No!

Friend, picking up Arab Sheik at airport: What impressed you the most about Americans?

Sheik, carrying his skis through the terminal: American salesmen!

Abraham received a vision in which God assured him he and Sarah would have a child who would inherit Abraham's spiritual legacy. Abraham and Sarah remained skeptical. He was 100 years old and she was 90. However, shortly after, Sarah conceived and their son, Isaac, was born. This event refuted Abraham's disbelief that God could fulfill the promise of an offspring to two long married and childless people. Unfortunately, Sarah became senile after the birth of her son.

Neighbor: Can I see baby Isaac?

Sarah: Later.

Neighbor, later: Can I see baby Isaac?

Sarah: Not Yet. Later.

Neighbor, much later: Okay, it's much later. Can I see baby Isaac now?

Sarah: No. You can only see baby Isaac when he cries.

Neighbor: Why do I have to wait until he cries?

Sarah: Because I forgot where I put him down.

Mother, examining her newborn son: Such tiny arms, he'll never be a boxer. Those small legs, he'll never be a runner either.

Husband: He'll never be a porn star either.

Husbands have this myth about sharing the birth experience. Unless you're passing a bowling ball through your mouth, I don't think so. Unless you're circumcising yourself with a chain saw, I don't think so. Unless you're opening an umbrella up your ass, I don't think so.

Husband, beaming over wife and new born son: Now, was that so hard, honey?

Wife: Smile as hard as you can. Now, stick your finger in each corner of your mouth. Stretch your lips as far as they well go.

Husband: So far, not too tough.

Wife: Pull them over your fucking head!

Wife: Give me three reasons why you can't change the baby in the middle of the night?

Husband: First, I'm sure he calls out "mommy." Second, you're so much better with him than I am. Finally, I've got an important meeting the day after next.

Husband: Dear God. You've got to help me. Please speak to me. My wife is going into labor.

God: Calm down. Is this her first child?

Husband: No! This is her husband.

Girl to friend: I was born by C-section. That was the last time I had my mother's complete attention.

One day, God tested Abraham's loyalties and commanded him to go to a nearby mountain top and sacrifice Isaac. Abraham ascended the mountain with Isaac, but didn't disclose the reason. Isaac did not question his father. Abraham made no special appeal to God to be released from this harrowing task. As he binds Isaac upon an altar and prepares to carry out God's command, an angel of God suddenly appears. The angel demands he cease the sacrifice because his faith in God is clearly established. Abraham is told to sacrifice a suffering goat caught in the brush, instead of his son.

Abraham, this modest person, who never aspired to wealth or power, is considered the most widely venerated human being who ever lived. He conceived a great simple idea of a single almighty God. Half the world now cherishes that concept. History will be forever transformed by his story as a servant of God.

CHAPTER TEN

ISAAC

A S ABRAHAM GREW older there was a pressing need to insure Isaac found a wife to continue the legacy promised by God. Guided by providence, he found an ideal match. Her name was Rebekah, a distant relative and a model of the very sensitivity that characterized Abraham himself. Rebekah, like her mother-in-law, Sarah, had trouble conceiving. They were childless the first twenty years of their marriage. They prayed fervently that God would bless them with a child.

Finally, their prayers were answered and Rebekah gave birth to twin sons, Esau and Jacob. According to custom, the oldest son, Esau, was to receive the birthright from Isaac. However, Rebekah carried a secret prophecy from God that Esau would serve Jacob. Her task was to manipulate matters so that Jacob would succeed Isaac. When the time arrived for Jacob to receive Isaac's blessing, she helped him dress like Esau. The aging and nearly blind Isaac gave Jacob the blessing that rightfully belonged to Esau.

Esau reacted angrily to the ruse committed against his blind father, and announced he would kill Jacob after Isaac died. Rebekah ordered

Jacob to flee. During his escape, Jacob dreamt of a ladder set up on the earth that reached heaven. There were angels of God descending upon its steps. God appeared at the top of the staircase and blessed Jacob. He confirmed the promise of land and offspring and affirmed his continual presence in Jacob's life.

Blindness was common in the Ancient World. The blind were one of a group to whom special protection was due. It was a good deed to help the blind and a violation to mislead them. Although blindness was attributed to various physical causes, including old age, as in Isaac's case, it could be interpreted as divine punishment.

BLIND-SIDED

Woman, dropping a coin in a beggar's cup: It must be dreadful to be lame! But, it must be worse to be blind?
Beggar: Your darn right, lady. When I was blind all I was getting was counterfeit money.

Hostess, at a Passover Seder, to a blind man: Hold your hand out for a piece of matzo.
Blind guest, feeling texture: Who wrote this shit?

Friend to Blind man: How did you like the cheese grater I gave you for your birthday?
Blind man: Great, man. That was the most violent book I ever read.

Czech eye doctor: Can you read this eye chart? CVKPMWXFCZ
Patient: Can I read it? I screwed her once.

Passerby to blind man: I just saw your guide dog lift his leg and piss all over your trousers. Then, you gave him a treat. You shouldn't reward him for that. The dog will never learn.
Blind man: I'm not rewarding him. I'm just trying to find his mouth so I can kick him in the ass.

Pretending blind man to Maitre D': This Lab is my guide dog. Table, please.

Maitre D': This way please.

2nd pretending blind man: This is my guide dog. Table, please.

Maitre D': That's no guide dog, that is a Chihuahua.

2nd pretending blind man: A Chihuahua! Those bastards gave me a Chihuahua.

THE BLIND DATE LOVE SCENE

Boy, at street corner waiting for his date: Are you Linda?

Linda: Are you Stuart?

Boy: Yes, I am.

Linda: Then, I'm not Linda.

Girl: I'm glad we spent the night together on our blind date. Tell me truthfully, am I the first girl you ever had?

Boy: It's possible. Were you at Disneyland in '99?

Man, on first blind date: Mind if I come inside?

Woman: Oh, no. I never ask a man inside on the first date.

Man: Okay, then. What about the last date?

Young man on a blind date in a chic Italian Restaurant: Hand me the menu, sweetie pie. I'll order. I'm an expert on good Italian dishes.

Girl, impressed: Sure, you order for us.

Man to waiter: We'll have the Giuseppe Spomdalucci.

Waiter: Sorry, sir. That's the proprietor.

Young man, rushing a blind date: If we should get married I would need to know how you feel about sex.

Date: Oh, I like to have it infrequently.

Young man: Was that one word or two?

Esau, the twin brother of Jacob, distinguished himself from his brother with a ruddy and hairy appearance, as well as his preference for hunting and the outdoor life,

Hunter, boasting: My friends, just watch this shot.

Friend: That bird just flew on.

Hunter: You are now viewing the good Lord's miracle. There flies a dead duck.

Hunter: Hello, 911? I'm hunting with a friend. He just dropped dead. What on earth should I do? Please help me!

Operator: Just calm down. I can help. First, let's make sure he's really dead.

Hunter: Okay. I can do that.

After a short silence the operator hears a shot.

Hunter: (returns to phone) Okay, Now What?

Two hunters came upon a rattlesnake and one was bitten on his penis.

Hunter: Quick. Race back out of the woods, find a doctor, and ask him what to do.

Doctor: It is critical that you suck out the venom for at least 10 minutes. It's the only solution.

Hunter: What did the doctor say?

Friend: He said you're going to die.

CHAPTER ELEVEN

JACOB

JACOB, NOW HEIR to Isaac's legacy, took refuge in Rebekah's brother's house. It is here, in his Uncle Laban's place, where he meets his two cousins. He shortly falls in love with Rachel, the youngest. Jacob, the trickster, who cheated his brother, Esau, has now met his match in Uncle Laban, who insists that giving away the younger daughter in marriage before the first born breaks with tradition. Jacob agrees to work for seven years for Rachel's dowry. Seven years later, Leah is still unmarried. Jacob agrees to marry Leah and to work another seven years for Rachael's hand in marriage.

Rachel proves herself to be a worthy partner for Jacob. Their wealth grows because of their care of her father's estates.

Jacob ultimately becomes the third patriarch of an ancient Hebrew family. He followed Abraham and Isaac. However, Jacob is the only patriarch who is also the ancestor of other nations. The twelve tribes sprang from his sons and grandsons. His name is mentioned more often in the Bible than Abraham's, making him a very significant being. When God gave Jacob a new name, Israel, it becomes the name of the nation itself.

ISRAEL, TODAY

American president, boasting: I am the proud president of 300 million people.
Israel president, responding: And, I'm the president of 5 million presidents.

Knesset member: Here's my solution to solve our economic problems. We'll declare war on the United States. We lose. The United States does what she always does when they defeat a country. Everything is rebuilt, highways, airports, bridges, schools, hospitals, factories and homes. They lend us money they know they'll never get back and send us food and medicines. Our problems will be over.
Another member: Sure, that's if we lose, but what if we should win?

Tourist at Wailing Wall: Excuse me sir, how often do you come here to pray?
Man: I have come every day for fifty years.
Tourist: What are you praying for?
Man: I pray for peace in this angry world. I pray for a world free of illness and disease. I pray for money and good health. I pray my wife and children will respect me. Every day I pray for something else.
Tourist: How do you feel about coming here for fifty years every day and praying for all those things?
Man: Like I'm talking to the wall.

Israeli: My friend, why did you buy an anti-Semitic newspaper? You should have bought the Jerusalem Post.
Tourist: The Post only has stories about anti-Semitism and all sorts of problems in Israel. I like to read about good news. This paper says the Jews have all the money. The Jews control the world banks. The Jews control the media and Hollywood. The Jews will agree to a Palestinian state when Hell freezes over. Nothing but good news in this paper!

Tour guide to Hadassah group: On this spot, at The Dome of The Rock, is where the Prophet Muhammad ascended to heaven.
Woman: When was that?
Tour guide: Ten fifteen.
Woman, looking at her watch: Ladies we just missed it by eleven minutes.

Texas tourist: I'm glad to meet an Israeli farmer. Tell me, how big is your farm?
Farmer: Five hundred feet by five hundred feet. How big is your farm?
Texas tourist: I could get in my car and drive from sunrise to sunset and never reach the end of my land.
Farmer: I once had a car like that.

CHAPTER TWELVE

JOSEPH

THE STORY OF Joseph is actually the story of the family of Jacob. Joseph is a key player. This is a tale of how an insignificant Israelite achieves success in the international arena, a sort of rags to riches plot. Joseph is Jacob's most favorite son. Because of Jacob's favoritism, all the brothers hated Joseph. One might have expected their anger to be directed against their father, but that was not the case.

The Bible relates one example of Jacob's partiality. The doting father made a special robe for his favorite son, referred to in the Bible as a "coat of many colors."

Customer to Tailor: In the name of heaven, my good man, it has taken you six weeks to make a pair of pants. Do you know it only took God to six days to create the world?
Tailor: So, look at it!

The saga of Joseph begins with his dreams in his early life. For ancient people, dreams were often seen as the way God communicated his purpose. For Joseph, dreams seemed to foretell future events. His brothers, in time, became utterly hostile and planned to kill him. Instead, they decided to make some money by selling him to passing traders. They planned to erase his memory from the family by faking his death and deceiving their father with Joseph's special robe stained with goat's blood. Jacob's unceasing grieving made it impossible for the brothers to ever forget Joseph.

Joseph was taken to Egypt and found himself employed in the house of two privileged servants of the pharaoh. He began to interpret their dreams.

Dreams were frequently regarded as vehicles of divine revelations. The skills of expert interpreters were required. The skills were thought to be God given. Interpreters constructed the pattern of future events from symbolic features of the dream. Joseph's talents were readily accepted at the Royal Court in Egypt.

In time, these successful interpretations came to the attention of the Pharaoh. Joseph began to interpret the Ruler's disturbing dreams. One dream predicted a calamitous seven-year famine after seven years of plenty. Joseph took it upon himself to outline the entire program that enabled Egypt to survive the famine. The Pharaoh appointed Joseph to oversee the program and he succeeded. The basic tenet of the plan was to store huge amounts of food during the years of plenty.

The predicted famine was widespread and devastating and people came from all over to buy food in Egypt from Joseph. The famine reached Jacob's family and he sent all his sons to Egypt to buy grain. He did not send Benjamin, the other son of his beloved Rachael. Joseph recognized his brothers immediately, but they did not know him. It was unimaginable to them that their brother could be in such a powerful position.

Joseph tested them several times to see if they were still cruel and thoughtless. He treated them poorly and announced he would hold one brother, Simeon, hostage, demanding they return with Benjamin. Eventually, Joseph relented, and returned their money hidden in their grains of wheat before they left Egypt.

On their return visit Joseph surprised his brothers. He sat them around a banquet table according to their ages. He arrested Benjamin on a ruse. All the brothers were upset. They worried about their father's reaction to Benjamin's imprisonment. One brother, Judah, pleaded with Joseph. He explained how horrible it would be for their father to lose another favorite child, and the pain of family disunity they had all suffered over the years. Judah, with words of selfless generosity, offered himself instead.

Joseph listened to the brothers' remorse and realized the family's relationships had changed. He identified with his brothers and the family's crisis and revealed himself to his astonished brothers.

Joseph invited his entire family to live in Egypt to escape the famine. Here, they prospered, acquiring land holdings and greatly increasing their wealth.

Before his death in Egypt, Jacob gave his blessings in a farewell address to his sons, who would become the ancestors of the twelve tribes of Israel. In time, Joseph also passed away, and was buried near the plot of his father.

CHAPTER THIRTEEN

MOSES

A NEW PHARAOH, PROBABLY Ramses II, came to power in Egypt. He was not bound by any law, and without provocation, decided the Israelites, once a welcome group during the time of Joseph, were now a threat. His first decree: Hebrew male children were to be killed at birth. Unable to hide her male child for any length of time, Moses' mother sought to evade the murderous edict. She bundled her infant into a waterproof container and lodged it among the reeds on the bank of the Nile River. This was a place where Pharaoh's daughter often bathed.

The princess' entourage came across the baby and brought the child to their mistress. Although she realized he was a Hebrew child she decided to raise him as her own. In effect, the King's daughter would house and support an enemy of the state. This was nothing else but high treason. The baby's sister, Miriam, was standing nearby and offered to find a Hebrew woman to breast feed the child. The baby's mother, Jachebed, close at hand, was summoned and hired as a nurse to feed and care for the child. The Pharaoh's daughter named the baby "Moshe," or "Moses." The child grew up to become the greatest leader and teacher in the history of the Jews. The young woman who saved his life, raised and educated him, was only referred to in the Bible as, "The Pharaoh's Daughter."

YOUNG MOSES

Moses had a princely upbringing, learning to read and write in the hieroglyphic system, while worshipping the multiplicity of Egyptian Gods. The Jewish Talmud tells a tale of his early days at Pharaoh's Court. One day three year old Moses snatched the crown from Pharaoh's head and put it on his own. The Pharaoh devised a test to see if Moses was aware of his transgression. Two plates were set before the child, one filled with gold, the other with red hot coals. If he chose the gold, death would be his reward. If the coals, he would be spared as one without knowledge of his acts. Moses took a coal and put it in his mouth, searing his tongue, which caused stuttering for the rest of his life.

MOSES FLEES EGYPT

At 40 years of age Moses could no longer remain silent while the Egyptians imposed various ruthless labor tasks making life unbearable for the Israelites. One day Moses walked among his people and witnessed the harsh treatment first hand. He noticed an Egyptian beating a Hebrew slave. Seeing nobody about, he struck down the Egyptian and hid his body in the sand. When Pharaoh learned of this through spies he sought to kill Moses. Moses was forced to flee Egypt and lived in the wilderness for another forty years. The once privileged man now found himself driven away from what had been an ideal life. Moses took refuge in the land of Midian, where he married Zipporah. The Midianites were also descendents of Abraham.

The Hebrew slave showed up for work one day at eight o'clock, one half hour late.

Slave Master, shouting: You should have been here at seven thirty!

Hebrew Slave: Why? What happened at seven thirty?

MOSES AND THE BURNING BUSH

One day, while Moses was tending his father-in-law's sheep, God revealed himself in a bush that appeared to be on fire, but was never consumed. God told Moses he is mindful of the Hebrews' suffering and intends to rescue them from the Egyptians. He will bring them to the land of milk and honey. Moses was also told he had been chosen to lead his people out of bondage. Moses was reluctant to agree to this responsibility. He argued his case with the Lord claiming he was not a good speaker. God wearily acquiesced and agreed that Moses' older brother, Aaron, would do the public speaking. They would both return to Egypt to persuade Pharaoh to let their people go. (Moses most likely kept in contact with his Hebrew family living in Egypt while growing up}.

Modern day crowds, watching a burning candle factory's flames that never seemed to go out, stood around all day singing, "Happy Birthday."

MOSES AND AARON MEET THE PHARAOH

The Lord warned them that trying times were ahead as the Pharaoh would be difficult to persuade. The brothers saw two living lions stationed at the entrance doors of the Pharaoh's palace. They prevented anyone from entering until a lion tamer was summoned to lead the lions away. Moses raised his rod and the lions bounded towards him and Aaron. Joyously, they followed them to the palace, jumping up and down as dogs before their master. Of course, Moses knew his way through familiar halls and they headed towards Pharaoh's throne room.

The guards stared in great awe, for the two of them resembled angels. Their countenances radiated splendor like the sun. The pupils of their eyes sparkled like stars. The terrified guards flung themselves down and prostrated their bodies before Moses and Aaron. The two representatives of the Children of Israel stepped before the Pharaoh and Aaron spoke, "The God of the Hebrews hath met with us and said, 'let my people go.'"

God knew Pharaoh's response in advance because God had to harden his heart to punish him. Aaron told Pharaoh he was dealing with the true God and there were a series of signs and destructive marvels to prove so. Suddenly, Moses' staff changed into a serpent at the Pharaoh's feet. Moses then placed his hand in his cloak. Lesions appeared and quickly disappeared. Pharaoh was intrigued by the performance, but probably dismissed it as sorcery.

The next morning the brothers stationed themselves at the Nile River where Pharaoh bathed. The stakes were now higher. Moses lifted his rod and turned the river to blood. The fish would die and the people would find it impossible to drink the water. Pharaoh turned and went back into his palace paying no heed to this. He had just witnessed the first of the ten plagues.

God: Moses, if Pharaoh will not let my people go, I'll send down a rain of frogs, a plague of locusts and flies, plus many other miserable things. I will turn the Nile to blood and, if Pharaoh's army pursues you in flight, I shall open a path for you in the Red Sea and close it again to drown his army.

Moses: That's incredible. Is there anything I can do to help?

God: Yes! I need an environmental impact statement before I can start.

THE TEN PLAGUES

1. River of blood.
2. Plague of frogs.
3. Dust turned to lice.

4. Plague of flies.
5. Killing of livestock.
6. Boils.
7. Hail and fire.
8. Plague of locusts.
9. Three days of darkness.
10. The death of the first born.

Several things occurred during this period. First, the Pharaoh kept refusing the pleas of Moses to let his people go. Then, the disdainful monarch issued a decree penalizing the Israelites by doubling the brick making time. It is important to note that God causes the stubborn Pharaoh to ignore the plagues. God wanted to use his most powerful curse last. One might say the Pharaoh's fate was, "In DeNILE."

The Pharaoh's stubbornness had cost his people dearly. After the tenth plague, he urged the Hebrews to leave. The entire series of plagues lasted one year. Pharaoh's urging the Israelites to leave gave Israel the right to become a nation. This was a claim not only supported by law, but by divine justification. The law was not the law of man, but the law of God.

THE FLIGHT OUT OF EGYPT

God promised Abraham his descendants would have their own lands, and now he was leading the Israelites out of Egypt. They were not allowed to travel the most direct route along the Mediterranean coast. They had to double back into the dessert. The Bible, without explanation, states God will lead them out by way of the wilderness. However, the explanation becomes obvious. God needed the time to teach the Israelites to behave morally and to prepare them to become a nation.

When Pharaoh permitted the Israelites to depart he had been convinced by Moses and Aaron they were going on a three day journey into the wilderness to offer sacrifices. Moses and Aaron hoped for a head start. As the three day period was coming to an end, the guards Pharaoh had sent noticed the people were not preparing to return. They were preparing for a sojourn into the dessert. The Israelites maintained they had been dismissed for good, but the guards thought otherwise. The Israelites had no choice. They killed some and wounded others. The surviving guards returned to Egypt and reported the insurgency to Pharaoh.

Now that the Children of Israel were gone, the Egyptians recognized how valuable they had been to their country. The Egyptians chased the fleeing Israelites into the dessert. The Egyptian forces were camped within sight of the Israelites. This was a terrifying scene to the people who thought they had finally escaped. They blamed Moses for the predicament they were in. Moses stood strong and with Aaron's help delivered comforting words. The people were told to prepare to witness the deliverance the Lord had promised. Moses assured them God would produce the miracle needed to guarantee their freedom.

Pharaoh, in his zeal to pursue the Israelites, sent six hundred chariots after them. The warriors were equipped with different sorts of weapons. The general custom was for two charioteers to take turns at driving to overtake their opponents. In this pursuit, the Pharaoh ordered three men assigned to each chariot to increase speed faster than had ever been achieved in the past.

FROM CHARIOTS TO AUTOMOBILES

Husband teaching wife to drive: Hit the brakes. For crying out loud!
Wife: The brakes don't work!
Husband: Grab the hand brake. We're going down this hill at 80 mph.
Wife: The hand brake just came off in my hand.
Husband: We're headed for a row of parked cars!
Wife: What should I do?
Husband: Try and hit something cheap!

A speeding car smashes through a guardrail, rolls down a cliff and
    lands upside down.

Arriving medic to driver: Are you drunk?
Driver: What do you think I am, a stunt driver?

Policeman to driver: I clocked you at 100 mph. Have you been
   drinking?
Driver: Yep! I had six or seven beers at a bar. They serve great
   margaritas. So, I guess I had three or four of them suckers. Then I
   stopped at my house and finished half a bottle of gin.
Policeman: Sir, you need to step out of the car and take a breathalyzer
   test.
Driver: Why? Don't you believe me?

Driver: Hello! I have just smacked into your parked car. Your brand
   new car's front was kissing my old Jalopy's ass. There are nosey
   people waiting here for a bus and watching me. They think I am
   writing this note to apologize and to leave my name, license, and
   phone number. In fact, I am not. Have a good day, you asshole
   sniffer.

Cop to Speeder: Do you have any ID?
Motorist: About What?

Priest to man hit by car: Do you believe in the Father, the Son and
   the Holy Ghost?
Man to crowd: I'm dying here and he's asking me riddles!

The nursing home patient was using her wheelchair as a make believe
   automobile to race through the halls.
Old man, jumps out of his room: Pull over ma'am. You were speeding.
   I need to see your driver's license.
Old lady, hands him a candy wrapper: Here it is officer.
Old man: I'll just give you a warning.
Old lady, caught speeding again: Sorry, officer.
Old man: Now I need to see your registration.
Old lady, hands him a library card: Here it is, sir.
Old man: This is your second and final warning.

Old lady, speeding again, as the old man jumps back into the hallway from his room, stark naked with an erection: Oh, NO! The breathalyzer test again!

Young Son: Why can't I use the car? I just got my driver's permit.-
Dad: First, bring up your grades. Study the Bible and get a haircut.
Dad, one month later: I'm really proud of you son. You've brought up your grades, you've studied the Bible diligently, but you didn't get your haircut.
Son: I learned from the Bible that Samson, Moses, Noah, and even Jesus, had long hair.
Dad: Yes. And they walked everywhere they went.

THE MIRACLE AT THE RED SEA

The Lord told Moses to hold his arm over the sea. The waters of the Red Sea parted and the Israelites walked across safely. Thousands of people, including their cattle, sheep and other animals needed considerable time to safely cross. Pharaoh's army was right on their heels into the sea, When his entire army entered the separated waters, the seas surged back with great force and his entire army was hurled into the raging water and perished. This extraordinary escape became part of the Israelite's psyche and the Israelites gained great faith in God and in Moses.

THE JOURNEY TO MOUNT SINAI TO RECEIVE THE TEN COMMANDMENTS

Entering the Promised Land was not as imminent as the people had expected. They complained to Moses and he tried to calm them by engaging in miracles orchestrated by God. But, God had a plan and was not irritated by their decreasing lack of confidence during this period. He waited three months before reuniting with the Israelites at Mount Sinai in the desert.

Moses communicated with God during a forty day stay on the mountain. During that time he received the Ten Commandments and committed the people to observing God's laws. When Moses returned to the people's camp he discovered that Aaron had supervised the construction of a golden calf made from melted gold rings, around which the people were praying and rejoicing.

Aaron claimed the people had grown impatient and had demanded new leadership during Moses' forty days away. He had built the golden calf to keep the peace. Moses was furious and smashed the tablets of law given to him by God. After Moses calmed down, he intervened with God on behalf of the Israelites. God agreed to replace the stone tablets.

According to Jewish tradition, the souls of Jews, even those still unborn, were present at Mount Sinai when God sealed his special covenant with the Chosen People.

THE TEN COMMANDMENTS
(THE SHORT VERSION)

COMMANDMENT ONE:
You shall have no other Gods before me. This guarantees the worship of one true God.

COMMANDMENT TWO:
Thou shall not make for yourself a graven image. This guards against worshipping idols.

COMMANDMENT THREE:
Thou shall not take the name of the Lord in vain. This protects against dishonoring God's name or using it in a meaningless or disrespectful way.

COMMANDMENT FOUR:
Remember the Sabbath day. Keep it Holy. This provides a special day each week for worship.

COMMANDMENT FIVE:
Honor your mother and father. This shows God's desire for close loving families whose members respect each other.

COMMANDMENT SIX:
Thou shall not kill. PERIOD.

COMMANDMENT SEVEN:
Thou shall not commit adultery. PERIOD.

COMMANDMENT EIGHT:
Thou shall not steal. PERIOD.

COMMANDMENT NINE:
Thou shall not bear false witness against thy neighbor. PERIOD.

COMMANDMENT TEN:
Thou shall not covet your neighbor or their possessions. This says, if we envy other people, the desire to do so can lead to breaking other commandments.

Moses stayed forty more days in heaven to learn and receive the Torah, the divine instructions of laws to live by. The Torah is one of the foundations of ancient and modern Judaism.

Just an aside: Man created more than thirty million laws to enforce God's ten commandments, and today's results are only marginal.

MY FAVORITE COMMANDMENTS

NUMBER SIX: THOU SHALL NOT KILL

Policeman: Is this the lifeless body of your husband? Is that a bloody 6 iron in your hand?
Wife: Yes to both your questions.

Policeman: How many times did you hit him with the club?

Wife: I'm not sure . . . maybe six, seven, nine. But, just put me down for six.

A search and medical team found an airplane that crashed at the top of a mountain. A lone survivor sat by a tree chewing on a bone and tossing it into a huge pile of bones. It appeared he had eaten the other passengers.

Survivor to rescue person: Thank God you're here. I am saved. Please don't judge me by what you see. I had to survive. Is it so wrong that I want to live? Is it so wrong?

Rescuer: I won't judge you for doing what was necessary to survive, but God, man, your plane only went down this morning.

NUMBER SEVEN: ADULTERY

Client to Lawyer: I want to sue my wife for divorce.

Lawyer: On what grounds?

Client: Because she says I'm a lousy lover.

Lawyer: That's why you want to divorce her?

Client: Of course not. I'm suing because she knows the difference.

New Bride: Why can't you tell me how many sex partners you've had?

Husband: If I tell you, you're going to get angry.

Bride: No, I won't. Cross my heart and hope to die.

Husband: Okay. Let me think. There was one, two, three four, you, six and seven.

The factory owner with roving eyes catches his fashion model robbing the safe. He can always smell opportunity when he sees it.

Man: I'm going to call the police.

Model: Please don't. I'll do anything you want. I won't tell your wife, I swear.

Man: Anything?

Model: Yes, anything.

Man: Take off your clothes and lie down on the couch in the back room.

He tried making love to her for two hours, but could not finish to save himself. He was an old man and it showed.

Man, as he comes off of her, exhausted: Look, it's not working. I'll have to send for the police.

Woman: Thanks Judge, for expediting my divorce based on the adultery laws. Now all I need is a "get."

Judge: What's a "get?"

Woman: It's my divorce under Jewish Law.

Judge: Oh, I see. It's like a bris.

Woman: Only in this case, you get rid of the entire schmuck.

Husband, catching best friend with his wife: You bastard! I've known you since school. You were my best man and my son's godfather. I gave you your first job. I lent you money. I went to all your family funerals. STOP DOING THAT WHEN I'M TALKING TO YOU!

Wife, in bed with her lover: Hurry, he's here. There's no time to get dressed. Quickly, go into the bathroom and I'll pretend I'm sleeping.

Husband, opens the bathroom door and sees a naked man clapping his hands in mid air: Who the hell are you?

Lover: I'm from the exterminating company. I'm trying to get rid of these pesky moths.

Husband: But you have no clothes on?

Lover, as he looks himself over: The little bastards!

Wife, picking up phone: How the hell should I know. It's 120 miles away.

Husband: Who was that?

Wife: Some mad dame wanting to know if the coast was clear.

NUMBER EIGHT

THOU SHALL NOT STEAL

Robber, to the customer in line behind him after robbing the bank: Did you just see me rob this bank.

Customer Yes!

Robber shoots and kills the witness and moves on to the next customer in line: Did you just see me rob the bank?

Customer: No, but my wife did.

Man at bar: Hey, buddy? You want to buy a ring?

Patron: What's it look like?

Man: Don't look now! See that drunken guy next to you who just passed out. He's wearing it.

Burglar freezes in his tracks: Who's that?

Voice: I can see you. Jesus can see you too.

Burglar throws his light onto parrot's cage: Did you say that?

Parrot: I can see you. Jesus can see you too.

Burglar: So what? You're just a parrot.

Parrot: I may be a parrot, but Jesus is a Doberman!

NUMBER TEN

THOU SHALL NOT COVET THY NEIGHBOR

Man to neighbor: Hey, do you like a woman with a big stomach?

Neighbor: Hell, no!

Man: What about a woman who has sagging breasts that almost touch her feet?

Neighbor: Hell, no!

Man: Do you like a woman who has hips as wide as a truck?

Neighbor: Hell, no!

Man: Well, then, keep your filthy hands off of my wife.

Wife: Our new neighbors are perfectly devoted to each other. He kisses her every time she goes out and even blows kisses to her from the window. Why don't you do that?

Husband: I hardly know the woman.

MOSES AND CIRCUMCISION

Circumcision is an operation to cut away the foreskin, an unneeded flap of skin on the penis. Jewish people usually do it when the baby is eight days old. To the ancient Hebrews, this was a sign of their special relationship with God. If the faithful worshipped Him and obeyed Him, He would be their God and they would be a special nation. The apostle Paul argued against circumcision and the leaders of the early church agreed with him.

Circumcision was enforced in the desert before the Hebrews were permitted to enter the Promised Land.

Circumcision, has, in fact, prevented Judaism from gaining its share of converts. Ninety-nine percent of potential converts head for the hills when the rabbi says, "and finally, all you have to do now is cut off the end of your penis."

Male guests, who witness the circumcision ceremony, may become sexually dysfunctional and often require counseling.

Moses: So, let me get this straight, My Lord. The Arabs get the oil, and we, your chosen people, get to cut off the tips of our what?

Five-year old boy at a urinal: You're thingy doesn't have any skin on it.

Friend: I've been circumcised. The skin was cut off.

Boy: Wow! When was it cut off?

Friend: When I was eight days old.

Boy: Did it hurt?

Friend: Did it hurt? Holy Crap. You bet it hurt. I didn't walk for a whole year.

Little girl gets her first period: Look what's happening, Johnnie?

Little Johnnie, with wide-open eyes: I'm no doctor, but it looks like someone just ripped your balls right out of their sockets.

MOSES AND KOSHER

It is said that eating Pork is like the sin of adultery for Jews. I have friends who've tried both and can't see the comparison.

God to Moses; It is the law. To keep a kosher home, never cook a calf in its mother's milk.

Moses: So, you're saying, we should never eat milk and meat together.

God: No. What I am saying is never cook a calf in its mother's milk.

Moses: Oh, Lord, forgive my ignorance. What you are really saying is, we should wait six hours after eating meat to eat milk, so the two are not in our stomachs together.

God: No, listen to me. I'm saying never cook a calf in its mother's milk.

Moses: Oh, Lord. I feel so stupid. You mean we should have separate sets of dishes for milk and meat, and separate sets of dishes for Passover, as well. If we make a mistake we must bury that dish.

God to Moses: Moses, do whatever you want!

Woman to Kosherlifeguard: You're an expert. Why was the bikini invented?

Lifeguard: To separate the dairy section from the meat section.

Orthodox Jewish man to Deli clerk: I'll have a half-pound of that corned beef, please.

Clerk: Sir, that's ham.

Man: Who asked you?

Jewish dietary laws should not be confused with the Jewish laws of dieting. Both involve widespread rationalization and cheating. Orthodox Jews will only eat food approved by a rabbinical council. Reformed Jews will also eat food approved by Martha Stewart.

MOSES SPENDS FORTY YEARS IN THE DESERT

The Promised Land was not yet around the corner. The Israelites remained at Mount Sinai for almost one year. Moses supervised the construction and erection of the Tabernacle during this time. The Tabernacle, conceived as a moveable shrine, was built so that it could be assembled, dismantled, and reassembled as the people moved from one place to another. This was the place where God was present among his people. This was the place where God could meet and communicate with them.

There was another possible reason Moses kept his people wandering around the desert for forty years. It is not mentioned in the Bible. Simply enough, he refused to ask for directions. He also managed to miss all the oil fields.

A Frenchman, an Italian, a Russian, a Mexican, and a Jew wandered in the desert for days.
Frenchman: I'm tired. I'm thirsty. I must have cognac.
Italian: I'm tired. I'm thirsty. I must have wine.
Russian: I'm tired. I'm thirsty. I must have vodka.
Mexican: I'm tired. I'm thirsty. I must have beer.
Jew: I'm tired. I'm thirsty. I must have diabetes.

THE DEATH OF MOSES

Moses had little choice. He had to learn his leadership skills via the power of the divine spirit. Moses' disciple, Joshua, was groomed by Moses to be the spiritual and military leader for The Children of Israel. When Moses was to die, Joshua was to lead the people into the Promised Land and fulfill God's promise to Abraham. It was God's will, when Moses was 120 years old, that Moses not enter the Promised Land, but see it afar from a high mountaintop.

Moses' achievements make him the founding father of Judaism. Moses abolished idol worship, banned magic from religious worship, instituted observance of the Sabbath, brought down the Ten Commandments, which became the cornerstone of western man's ethical life, and was an unsurpassed leader of men. He led his people on history's greatest detour to the threshold of the Promised Land. It's safe to say he cast a towering shadow across the centuries to our time.

On the eve of his death Moses delivered a series of farewell addresses to the people. He expounded upon the law and its requirements for living in the new land. He offered a personal good-bye and blessed all the Tribes. He died full of life and vigor. Moses was the greatest prophet and his name is mentioned numerous times in the Old Testament. God gave the laws and his teaching to the world through Moses, and now it fell to Joshua to continue the work Moses had begun.

CHAPTER FOURTEEN

JOSHUA

MOSES HAD BEEN a patient statesman, but Joshua was only a blunt warrior. Moses had ruled bloodlessly, "inventing" interviews with God, while Joshua ruled by the second law of nature. The superior killer survives. Due to Joshua's realistic and unsentimental beliefs, the Jews "took their land."

Joshua led the Children of Israel across the Jordon River to the Promised Land. On the same day he erected twelve memorial stones to represent the twelve tribes that crossed the river. The territory, at that time, was called Canaan, and its people were called Canaanites. Their cities were well developed and each had its own king and army. These city kingdoms often battled each other. All the populations were descendants of Ham, Noah's youngest son, genetically aligned with modern world Arabs. These ancient people worshipped many Gods and it became necessary for the Israelites to conquer the Canaanites before they could live in peace in the Promised Land.

Joshua's first victory was the capture of Jericho, perhaps the most famous battle in the Bible. This had a military and psychological effect upon the Children of Israel. However, warfare waged on for seven years until Israel finally conquered the entire region, demolishing all the city kings.

He was at least seventy years old by then, and could now distribute the conquered land among the tribes. This was his system. Two urns were set up. One contained the individual names of all the tribes. The other held the individual names of the twelve districts to be awarded. As the name of a tribe was drawn out of the first urn, a corresponding district name was drawn out of the second.

When the match-ups were completed, Joshua issued ordinances describing the laws and rules to the new property owners. For example, passage into the woods between properties would be free to the public at large. Everyone was permitted to gather up bits of wood for cooking on any property. For grafting purposes, twigs from any fruit tree or vegetable plant could be cut from anybody's property. Olive trees were the exception. All sources of water, wherever located, belonged to everyone.

Joshua decreed that a known hardy shrub be planted between districts to maintain their boundaries. The plant root, once firmly established, was almost impossible to kill, even if ploughed over. The plant would develop new roots and grow back stronger than ever.

Joshua called all the tribe leaders together to encourage them to drive away all remaining enemies in their districts. He reminded them to worship only God and to do all that God commanded. He retired from leading the Israelites after twenty-eight years of service marked by war and peace, and shortly after departed from this life.

CHAPTER FIFTEEN

ANCIENT HEBREW FAMILY LIFE

AMID SWIRLING CYCLES of conflict, victory, defeat, destruction, and reconstruction, the Hebrew people patiently pursued their everyday lives. Archeologists found a monotonous succession of devastations deep in the earth as stark evidence the ancient times were an age of violence, pillage, and sudden death. Virtually every generation saw its homes sacked and burned by invading enemies. Had we lived then, we would have prayed fervently to God or any idol of our choice.

The first houses of the early biblical period were woven tents set up near a source of water. However, small villages and larger towns and cities grew with the development of cisterns and water systems. It was possible for people to live further away from the rivers and streams. At this time, sharp durable tools of iron replaced the farmer's crude sickles of flint and wood. The economy depended primarily upon agriculture and the changing seasons controlled the rhythms of life. The Israeli farmer did not live on his scanty acreage. He lived in the nearest fortified town where he was afforded some measure of protection against enemy raids. Cities and towns were typically overcrowded. Since homes had to be built within the available space, bizarre architectural angles and shapes have been found in the ruins.

The simplest homes were constructed of sun dried mud bricks with waterproofing plaster walls. The floors were generally packed with earth. The windows were small and closed with lattices. One could look out, but not in. In later years, a second story was added and small central courtyards were designed. Usually, the Hebrew family inhabited the second story and used the ground level for work and storage space.

Furniture was sparse, but there were commonly used items like a mat for a bed, a table, and a lamp. Burning olive oil produced light. Clay pots were used for serving. Large vessels were used for food preparation. The preparation of bread, a staple, required a stone grinder and an oven. Each home needed a large stone mortar for crushing food.

Israeli craftsman: Could I have Sunday off. It's my golden wedding anniversary?
Boss: Do I have to put up with this every fifty years?

Shop sign: Stop looking at the sundial. It's earlier than you think.

Carpenters constructed the doors and windows of houses, road carts, and occasionally fashioned a table or chest. Metal workers manufactured the farm implements plus other tools and weapons. Potters produced items for cooking, serving and storing foods. Archaeologists use pottery chards most often for carbon dating. According to their techniques, a simple potter's wheel came into use about 3000 BC.

Tanners made leather for shields, helmets and other military articles. They produced sandals, belts, and storage skins for wine, water and the like. Jewelers worked with gold and silver. Engravers produced signet rings and seals of various types. Luxury items were carved from ivory and wood. There were perfumers who brought their skills to a community that bathed infrequently.

Woman: Does that perfume really work?
Clerk: I wouldn't use it if you were only bluffing.

Weavers made the clothing and dyers added color. There is an erroneous belief that Israelites dressed like modern Bedouins. In reality, the basic garment for the male was a short wrap around skirt made of cloth or leather held together by a belt, which also served to hold weapons and valuables. A short-sleeved garment, much like today's t-shirt, usually covered the upper trunk. Cloaks were long and close fitting. At night they served as a bed and blanket. Shoes were always sandal styled. Feminine attire was virtually identical to the men's, except they never wore a short skirt and they often had a long narrow scarf draped over their head.

CLOTHES MAKE THE MAN

Customer: Do you make custom suits?
Tailor; You've come to the right place. First, digital cameras take pictures of your every muscle. Then, we download the pictures into a special computer to build up your image. After that we shear sheep in Australia to get the very best cloth. We contact Japan for the very best linings from their silk worms. Then we ask Japanese deep-sea divers to get the pearly buttons.
Customer: But, I need the suit for a Bar Mitzvah.
Tailor: When?
Customer: Tomorrow.
Tailor: You'll have it!

Man to tailor: Listen, Pincus, my friend and I want the darkest of dark custom-made suits.
Pincus: I stock the blackest cloth on the market. In fact, this is the stuff they use for nuns' habits.
Several weeks later the men are walking in the street wearing their new black suits. As two nuns walk by one man gets close enough

to a nun and quickly matches his black color with her habit. He becomes very angry and mutters something to his friend.

Nun #1: What did the man want?

Nun #2: I don't know. He looked at my habit and said something in Latin.

Nun #1: What did he say?

Nun #2: He said, "Pincus fuctus."

Customer in army navy surplus store: Do you sell any camouflage jackets?

Clerk: Yes, we do. But, we can't seem to find any of them.

The 90-year-old flasher streaked through the dining room in the nursing home.

Retired tailor: Whatever he's wearing, he should never wear it again until he has it pressed, for God's sake.

Man to friend: I like your new suit.

Friend: It was a present from my wife. I came home early last night, and to my surprise it was hanging over a chair in our bedroom.

CLOTHES MAKE THE WOMAN ALSO

Clothing manufacturer addressing men's club: I have invented a bra that keeps women's breasts from jiggling and preventing their nipples from pushing through the fabric when cold weather sets in.

After the meeting, a large group of men took the guy outside and kicked the shit out of him.

CHAPTER SIXTEEN

SEX IN THE CITY

A WEDDING REPRESEN-TED the culmination of long discussions between the two families. The two fathers negotiated the terms of the marriage contract, including the amount of the dowry.

Father to friend: My daughter is getting married tomorrow and I promised a dowry of 25,000 shekels. Now, half the dowry is missing.

Friend: So what? One usually pays only half of the promised dowry at the beginning of the wedding.

Father: I know, but that's the half that's missing.

There was a double standard with regard to sexual behavior. Premarital virginity was incumbent only upon the females. If a husband proved his wife was not a virgin at the time of their marriage, the wife would be stoned. Prostitutes suffered the same penalty. It is not difficult to imagine the patriarchal society that concocted these rules. Certainly, there is no evidence these are God's laws. The Lord's interests were carved out in stone and well defined. "Thou shall not kill." God would never approve of a stoning because some misguided individual decided to spread her legs for a few shekels.

Jesus: What's going on here?
Man in the crowd: That woman is a prostitute and we are going to stone her.
Jesus: Let those who are without sin cast the first stone.
Everyone in the crowd disbanded except for a middle-aged woman. She lifted a heavy stone, took aim, and hit the prostitute on her head, killing her.
Jesus: Mother, sometimes you really piss me off.

Priest to man: I'm sorry to see a good Catholic like you coming out of a brothel.
Man: I'm not a Catholic. I'm Jewish.
Priest: But, I just saw you cross yourself?
Man: Listen, Father. Whenever I come out of a place like that I always check four things . . . my spectacles, my testicles, my watch and my wallet.

Guest to hotel concierge: I want three call girls, a blond, a tall black woman, and an oriental virgin in a red dress with high black boots. Send them along with the best marijuana and a gram of cocaine. Call me back to confirm this order, and tell me when I can expect them.

Concierge, a half hour later: Hello. This is the concierge calling back. I have the marijuana, the cocaine, the blond and the tall black woman. I haven't been able to locate the oriental virgin in a red dress with knee-high boots, yet.

Guest, thinking: I see. Look, in that case, just cancel the order and send up a prune Danish and a cup of coffee.

Customer to Madame: I'll pay $500 for a girl who will just lay still.
Madame: For that kind of money you can have the wildest girl in the house.
Customer: No, thank you. I'm not horny, just homesick.

The front door bell rang at the brothel. A girl answered the door. A
   guy without arms or legs sat there in a wheel chair.
Girl: What the hell do you think you're going to do here?
Guy: I rang the doorbell, didn't I?

LOVE AND MARRIAGE

Man, talking to God: If a married Jewish man is walking alone
in the forest, and he expresses an opinion without anyone around to
hear him, tell me, My Lord, is he still wrong?

A couple, celebrating their twenty fifth wedding anniversary went
back to the same hotel, same room and same bed they had visited on
their honeymoon.
She: What were you thinking 25 years ago on this night?
He: I was thinking, I'd like to fuck your brains out.
She: So, what are you thinking now?
He: I think I did it.

Wife: Honey, if you want to have sex with me, squeeze my left breast
   one time. If you don't, squeeze my right breast one time.
Husband: Now, if you want to have sex with me, pull on my penis
   one time. If you don't, then pull on my penis one hundred times.

CHAPTER SEVENTEEN

FINALLY, DEATH

THE BIBLICAL CONCEPT of death is complex. The popular notion was you died because God was punishing you. Thus, it was believed, God alone had the authority to terminate life. Those responsible for executing criminals or causing accidental deaths acted on God's behalf. Burial took place without delay, often on the same day. Neither embalming or cremation was allowed. The burial place was apart from the family dwelling. There was a tradition of demonstrative mourning. There were groups of women who were professional mourners as part of the funeral procession.

Onlooker #1 at funeral procession: Who died?

Onlooker #2: Big Angelo's girlfriend.

Onlooker #1: She was so young. What did she die of?

Onlooker #2: Gonorrhea.

Onlooker #1: Gonorrhea! That's impossible. Nobody dies from Gonorrhea.

Onlooker #2: You do, when you give it to Big Angelo.

Widow: Hello. Obituary ad section? How much does it cost to have an obituary printed?

Clerk: It's five dollars a word. The telephone number is free.

Widow: Sounds expensive.

Clerk: We do have a special this week. A five-word ad for twenty dollars.

Widow: Okay. Write this down. "Cohen dead. Cadillac for sale. 645-3900."

Wife to husband: I have just one request from this hospital bed.

Husband: Anything at all.

Wife: In sixty years of marriage we never had oral sex and I want to die knowing what it feels like.

The husband closed the door and complied with her wishes. To everyone's amazement, she was well enough within a week to go home. Her husband broke down in tears.

Wife: What's wrong? What are you crying about?

Husband: I just realized I could have saved Eleanor Roosevelt.

Husband: My medical exam showed I was certain to die from a rare virus within twenty-four hours. I want to make love to you as often as I can manage long into the night.

Wife: That's easy for you to say. You don't have to get up in the morning.

Father: Son, here lies a lawyer and an honest man.

Son: How can there be room for two men in that one little grave?

Man to friend: When I die, I want to go like my grandfather, in his sleep. Not screaming like the other passengers in his car.

CHAPTER EIGHTEEN

SAMSON

AFTER THE DEATH of Joshua, and for the next four hundred years, the Israelites slowly began to forget about God. They worshipped idols and other false gods like those of the neighboring countries. The twelve tribes fought against each other, more concerned about themselves individually, than about the nation of Israel as a whole. There were times when the Israelites had difficulties with enemies such as the Philistines, the Hittites and several other groups. During these times, they called upon God for help. God reacted by appointing a judge to lead them to victory. The Book of Judges relates what happened during this period.

Samson, one of the less important judges, but one of the greatest heroes of the time, was appointed. He had super human strength and a gigantic body. The Old Testament details how Samson single handedly killed one thousand Philistines with the jawbone of an ass.

Samson fell in love with a woman named, "Delilah." The Philistines offered Delilah much money to find out what made Samson so strong. She coaxed Samson into divulging his secret. His strength was in his hair. He would lose his strength if his head were shaved.

The enemy shaved his head while Samson slept. His God given strength departed. They also took the opportunity to blind him by poking out his eyes. He was then thrown into prison to work at hard labor.

As time went by, the Philistines were disinterested in Samson's new hair growth. During a festival, Samson was brought into a temple to be mocked by the people. Standing between two pillars, he prayed to God for the strength to push them to the ground. As the walls and the ceiling fell, thousands of people were killed and, so was Samson.

Customer to Barber: Cut my hair so it's all different lengths around the front and the back. Make a strange spiky bit of hair on top and some bald patches here and there.
Barber: I don't think I can do that.
Customer: Why not? You did it the last time I was here.

Barber: And how would you like your hair cut today?
Customer: In silence.

Customer to Barber: Don't put that smelly stuff on my hair. My wife will think I just came from a whore house.
Guy in next chair: You can put it on my hair. My wife doesn't know what a whore house smells like.

EXTRA STRENGTH FORMULA

Samson: I have a question, My Lord. At age 20 I could bend my erect penis back about 10 degrees. At 30, about 25 degrees. At 60, about 90 degrees. Now, I'm 100 years old and I can bend it back more than 120 degrees.
God: So what disturbs you, my son?
Samson: I know you made me strong, but is it normal for my arm to keep getting stronger as I age?

CHAPTER NINETEEN

THE KINGS

SAUL, A STRUGGLING KING

S AMUEL, THE LAST judge, yielded to the peoples' demands for a king and appointed Saul as Israel's first king. It was immediately apparent he was an erratic ruler. He was brave and idealistic, but his judgment was poor. Samuel announced that God had rejected Saul as a king over Israel, but Saul refused to abdicate his throne. Instead, he waged a war he could not possibly win and fell upon his own sword after a hopeless battle against the Philistines.

There is no evidence Saul made any appreciable changes in the nation's internal structure, but he did leave an important legacy for Israel. David, his son in law, would become the greatest king in the history of Israel.

DAVID, THE UNITER

The rise and fall of Saul, the first king of Israel, illustrated what the office ought not to be. The king must follow God's will and keep the commandments. These standards must always supercede the quest for power and glory. When David was king of Israel, it had a brave and dedicated leader. Sometimes, he was blinded by personal ambition, but, nonetheless, he accepted God's wishes and unified the people.

David began his assent to the throne as a young shepherd boy who was anointed by Samuel to become the next king of Israel. David was introduced into Saul's palace as a musician who could calm Saul's nervous episodes.

A Philistine giant, Goliath, challenged the Israelites to send one man to fight him alone, rather than have the two armies slug it out. No one volunteered, except David. He believed God would save him from harm. He hit Goliath on the forehead with his slingshot. The giant fell to the ground. David rushed over and killed him with his sword. David was now a hero in the eyes of the Israelites.

Archeologist to museum curator: I found a mummy 3,128 years old who committed suicide.

Curator: How do you know the mummy's exact age?

Archeologist: Because he was clutching a piece of papyrus in his hand which read, "50,000 shekels on Goliath."

King Saul grew jealous of David. David's life was threatened even after he married one of the king's daughters. David went into hiding until he learned of Saul's death on the battlefield. David quickly returned to Israel and the people proclaimed him King.

Unlike Saul, David commanded a unified army capable of winning frequent battles. One battle not only routed the Philistines completely from their land, but Jerusalem was captured and established as the capital of Israel.

David's victory was significant because the Ark of the Covenant, in the arms of the Philistines, was recovered. This chest contained the tablets of the laws given to Moses by God at Mount Sinai. God's presence was now safely in the Israelite's possession.

David's ability to re-establish the ark as the focal point of a religious center helped him create Jerusalem's reputation. He unified the tribes, he reduced the power of neighboring states and for a brief moment in history, the tiny empire of Israel was the strongest force in the region.

To thank David for building a temple to worship and honor God, the Lord decided he would create a dynasty, guaranteeing that David's descendants would always inhabit the earth. David was a skillful leader, but his private life was often in disarray. There were difficult years with his rebellious sons, and more important, was his penchant for multiple marriages.

The Bible names only one of his wives, Bathsheba, his favorite, stolen from another man. Thus, he violated the 7th commandment, "Thou shall not commit adultery." The Bible recorded that David truly repented, unlike Saul, who refused to acknowledge his sins.

Despite his failures, David is remembered as a beloved king who protected his people from their enemies and enhanced their everyday lives. He died at the age of seventy.

SOLOMON, THE GOLDEN AGE

Solomon, David and Bathsheba's son, succeeded his father to the throne. King Solomon's reign was known for its prosperity, prestige, and grandiose projects. Solomon possessed the God given gift of wisdom. The most famous example: Two women, each of whom had a newborn child, came before him to adjudicate their problem. One of the infants had died, and each woman was claiming the living one as her own. Solomon proposed the child be divided into two, knowing the real mother would recoil at the suggestion. She did, and the child was returned to its rightful mother.

It was Solomon's personal genius that preserved the powerful nation he acquired from his father. He consolidated his power by ruthlessly eliminating his opponents one by one and appointing his trusted friends to key positions. In an ancient near eastern empire this was the best means of establishing a stable government. Like other empire builders, Solomon maintained his power using military might. The country was destined to become an important center because of its strategic location for trade by land and sea. Solomon fulfilled his kingdom's commercial destiny and brought it to its greatest heights.

Solomon proved to be an excellent administrator. He organized his kingdom into districts for taxation purposes and created labor teams for building a planned massive temple in Jerusalem. This amazing building would be used as a meeting place where God's spirit and man could come together. Solomon built new cities, including buildings in outlying areas for grain storage, and housing for corps of fighting chariots and large cavalry forces

Solomon taught his people the value of law and order and lured the population away from the discord of war to the benefits of industry and peace. He became a trading partner with Africa, Arabia and surround the areas, and attracted the Queen of Sheba from Arabia to visit his developing kingdom. She compared his empire to those of the ancient near east and concluded the God of Israel was responsible for his successes.

Unfortunately, as with his predecessors, Solomon was not a perfect human being. For political reasons, he married many foreign women, who were idol worshippers, and the practice spread to his people. Unwisely, he encouraged the Israelites by building places of worship for the idols. God responded by deserting Solomon. He sent political adversaries to undermine the King. The empire began to crumble, and after his death some of the tribes deserted Rehoboam, Solomon's son and rightful heir. The Kingdom could no longer be sustained. Solomon, the third King of Israel, was also the last.

After Solomon's death, Israel was divided into two lesser kingdoms, the Monarchies of Israel to the north and Judah to the South. They survived for many centuries.

CHAPTER TWENTY

THE PROPHETS

THE AGE OF the prophets is one of the finest in Israeli history. It was a time when the Lord worked directly with his wayward chosen people to give them evidence of his unmistakable presence and tokens of deep love.

There is no comprehensive definition of an Israeli prophet. Any person included in the category had some kind of a close relationship with God via direct divine messages, visual sightings or dreams. The messages from God were frequently unsolicited. Occasionally, a prophet would be asked directly by another if there was a message for him or her. In general, prophets were feared. Many achieved profound insights into the relationship between God and his people, and many delivered unpalatable messages, thought to be unauthentic messages from God and were liable to suffer humiliations. In spite of their status in the community, there is no evidence they enjoyed an official role in either the religious or in the political establishment.

Ancient Israeli prophets were not unlike modern day fortunetellers, prognosticators, soothsayers, tarot card readers, mediums, astrologists, and Chinese fortune cookies. However, one thing differentiates them from today . . . their predictions were divinely inspired revelations. They predicted future events with total assurance. Surprisingly, their work often stood the test of time.

We now focus on six prophets of particular importance in the Old Testament.

1. ELIJAH

Elijah, famous for his fiery words, would appear without warning. He would deliver messages from God to Israel's leaders and then disappear. While his prophecies were numerous, his most famous one was a contest with the prophet of Baal. Baal, the Canaanite God of Rain, worshipped by King Abash and his wicked wife, Jezebel, who brought this false idol into life, built an altar and placed a sacrifice upon it. Elijah also placed a sacrifice on the altar. They agreed the true God would send down fire to burn the sacrifices, thus proving who was the true God. The prophet of Baal prayed for hours, but no fire came. Elijah than shocked the onlookers by pouring water over his sacrifice. The Lord sent a fire so hot it burned the altar as well as the sacrifice.

Elijah never did die. Instead, he rode to heaven in a whirlwind with fiery horses and a chariot. Elijah transcended the Old and the New Testaments. In the New Testament, Jesus called Elijah by another name, John, the Baptist.

Jews remember Elijah's reputation for appearing and disappearing until this day during the Passover Seder. A glass of wine is set for him and a door is opened to allow him a spiritual visit.

Teenager to Fortune Teller: Could I speak to my grandmother? I want to know if she's happy in heaven.

Fortune Teller: Of course, just listen.

Grandmother: Don't worry about me, darling. I am very happy here in heaven.

Teenager: That's wonderful. There is one more thing I have to know. When did you learn to speak English, Bubba?

2. ISAIAH

God called upon Isaiah to be a prophet during the kingdom of Judah. Isaiah's message focused on trusting God, the Holy King of Heaven and Earth, during the wars and revolts Judah was experiencing. He specifically warned the people that God was more interested in honest living than in animal sacrifices, for He was hateful of sin and idol worship.

Isaiah is also one of the Major Prophets who appear in Christian tradition. He seemed to be waiting for the coming of the Messiah more than any other prophet. Probably, his most well known prophesy describes the picture of a suffering Savior and seems to describe the life and ministry of Christ with stunning accuracy. Jesus began his public appearances in Nazareth by reading from Isaiah's scriptures.

The religious school class stopped in front of a cage shared by a lion and a calf.

Teacher to zookeeper: How long have you kept the lion and the calf together?

Keeper: Over one year.

Teacher to students: See, Isaiah's prophecy has come true. A lion and a calf can share the same cage.

Teacher to keeper: How have you managed to do this?

Keeper: Oh, easily. Every day we put in a fresh calf.

3. JEREMIAH

One of the greatest Old Testament prophets was one of the most unpopular. The messages God gave Jeremiah made the people angry. He told them God was judging their evil acts and a great power from the North would come and conquer them. Jeremiah spent much of his life in prison or hiding from angry leaders. Eventually, he was permitted to live in communities, but forbidden from uttering God's terrible prophesies any more. Instead, Jeremiah wrote God's words, and others read them aloud. This ploy was quickly put down.

Nebuchadnezzar, King of Babylon, arrived with his army and surrounded Jerusalem. The people tried to hold out against the invading forces, but Jeremiah's prophecies were fulfilled. Jerusalem was destroyed, including Solomon's beautiful temple. Many people returned to Babylon as exiles. Many others, including Jeremiah, fled to Egypt, to create new lives. Jeremiah continued to urge the Israelites to turn away from idolatry and to worship God again.

Although Jeremiah's prophecies were about bad things that would continue to haunt the Hebrews, he also wrote about a new covenant with God forgiving their sins. This covenant is mentioned in the New Testament.

4. EZEKIEL

This important prophet lived in exile in Babylon. He foretold the Jews would return to Jerusalem and rebuild the temple. He taught God was with them in Babylonia just as much as he had been in Israel. Ezekiel said they must obey God wherever they were. He promised the people that enemies of Israel, the Babylonians and the Egyptians, deserved to be punished and accountable to God. He died in Babylonia and never saw the Temple in Jerusalem restored.

5. DANIEL

Daniel was a young man when Babylon defeated Israel. He was trained to serve as an interpreter of the king's dreams in the Babylonian court of King Nebuchadnezzar. After the King's death, Daniel continued to serve the new King Balthazar in the same way. During a banquet, mysterious handwriting appeared on the wall, and Daniel was the only person who could read it. He told the new king his kingdom would be destroyed. Balthazar died the same day Persia captured Babylon.

The new Persian ruler, Darius, recognized Daniel's abilities and made him one of the top three officials in the country. Several jealous

Persians persuaded Darius to decree that only he, Darius, could speak with God. If one disobeyed the law he would be thrown into a den of lions. Thus, Daniel was entrapped as he fulfilled his obligation to pray to God three times a day. Darius, despite his feelings of concern for Daniel, capitulated, and Daniel was thrown to the lions.

In contrast to Darius, who spent a torturous night fearing the worst, Daniel, who had been protected by an angel, was unharmed. Daniel was returned to his position of power and the conspirators were sentenced to the same fate they had intended for Daniel. The king wrote a new law: His people were to fear the God of Daniel.

The young man was applying for a job as an assistant lion tamer. The circus owner took him to a cage to observe the head lion tamer. She was a beautiful woman dressed in a skimpy costume, beckoning the lion to come and lick her exposed tits as she lay quietly on the floor.

Owner: Well, do you think you can do that?

Young man: I'm sure I could. But first, you'll have to get those damn lions out of there.

6. JONAH

Jonah was a minor prophet but his story is important. It is more about his personality than the value of his prophesies. He fled from God on a ship when asked to spread God's message. God retaliated and created a major storm, which threatened to sink the ship. Jonah admitted to the sailors that he was the cause of God's wrath and the storm. In order to save themselves, the sailors threw him overboard.

A great fish swallowed him and prevented him from drowning. Only when he was in the belly of this great fish did Jonah offer a prayer to The Lord asking for forgiveness. After three days the fish spit him out near the shore. His faith was restored and Jonah spent the rest of his days as a faithful messenger for God.

OTHER FISH TALES

Man: I caught a fish so huge, it must have weight at least fifty pounds.

Friend: I caught an antique lamp. It had a date of 300 BC engraved on it, and a candle was still lit.

Man: I'll tell you what. We have to stop bragging to each other. Let's compromise. I'll say my fish only weighed five pounds, and you will blow out your candle.

Sign under a mounted fish: If I had only kept my mouth shut I wouldn't be here now.

Customer: I don't like the looks of that catfish.

Clerk: Lady, for looks you don't buy catfish, you buy goldfish.

Fishing Pal to Buddy: It seems the size of the fish you caught changes according to the person who's listening to you.

Buddy: Well, I never like to tell someone more than I think they'll ever believe.

The diver enjoyed exploring the deep ocean in his expensive diving gear. Suddenly, a stranger appeared wearing only a bathing suit.

The diver wrote on his waterproof pad: How did you get here with just a bathing suit? It cost me a fortune to get this deep.

The swimmer grabbed the waterproof pen and pad: I'm drowning you dumb schmuck!

Lady oyster to a friend: I met the lobster at the bottom of the ocean and we had our first date. He looked deeply into my eyes and placed all his arms around me. Then, he . . .

Friend: Then, he what?

Lady oyster, with a look of horror: Oh! My God! They're gone. My pearls are gone!

St. Peter to new arrival: Sorry, but you've told too many lies to be permitted to enter heaven.

New arrival: Have a heart. Remember, you were once a fisherman yourself.

CHAPTER TWENTY-ONE

KEEPERS OF THE JEWISH FAITH

THE HIGH PRIEST

THE HIGH PRIEST was a person attached to the service of God. He lived in a sanctuary, God's house. He dressed in elaborate and beautiful clothing reflecting the glory of God. In the days of the monarchy, a high priest and his assistants, the secondary priests beneath him, led the priesthood in Jerusalem.

Nearing the end of the Old Testament, when Israel no longer had a king, the High Priest had great powers because religion and government were closely entwined. He was a direct descendant of Aaron, the brother of Moses and, once consecrated, was the spiritual leader of the Israelites for life.

RABBI, TEACHER

Rabbis were not a separate caste of people. In ancient times, they were ordained to be authorities in the study and practice of Jewish law. They regularly socialized with the common people as they too came from ordinary people. They generally worked part time in a trade, as a carpenter, cobbler and the like.

Within his community, the Rabbi functioned as an interpreter of Torah, a judge, a mystic (with the ability to talk to the deceased), a social worker and a health care advocate. In modern times you might compare this to a public advocator or a community organizer, not unlike Barack Obama. (Except for the Torah, and talking parts)

Rabbis embraced an all knowing, all wise, just, merciful and loving God who supervised the lives of individuals and decreed fates while also allowing free will to chose between good and evil. The Rabbis taught salvation would come to all observant Jews, and one day the Messiah would come to earth.

RABBIS AND THEIR SYNAGOGUES

The emergence of the synagogue was a revolutionary development in the history of Judaism. Synagogues not only represented a new concept of religious observance, but also a new form of communal institution. The nature of official worship shifted dramatically with prayer and study replacing sacrifice as the way to serve God. The synagogue was open to all and the community was no longer confined to a small group of priests. The masses of people were no longer relegated to outer courtyards during ceremonies, as was the case at the temple in Jerusalem.

Despite its importance in Jewish history, the origins of the synagogue are shrouded in mystery. Archaeologists have discovered over one hundred structures in Israel dating to the first century, BC. No matter its mysterious origins, the synagogue has become a fully developed communal institution in most Jewish communities around the world.

Rabbi's son: How do you know what to say when you write your sermon?
Rabbi: Easy. God tells me.

Son: Then why do you keep crossing things out?

Rabbi to Congregation: I found a letter in my mailbox. A single piece of paper that just read, "SCHMUCK." In the past, people have written to me who have forgotten to sign their note. This is the first time I have received a letter from a person who signed it and forgot to write the letter.

Reform Rabbi: Why don't you allow the men and women of your congregation to sit together as they can in my synagogue?
Orthodox Rabbi: I don't mind them sitting together. But, with the kind of sermon I give, I can't have them sleeping together.

Hebrew school student: Rabbi, when you are not making speeches or leading some prayers, what else do you do? I'm really thinking of becoming a Rabbi some day.
Rabbi: Listen, kid. You don't want to become a Rabbi. You want to be a temple president.

IRS: Hello? Is this Rabbi Cohen?
Rabbi: It is.
IRS: Do you know a Joseph Levy?
Rabbi: I do.
IRS: Did he donate ten thousand dollars to your synagogue?
Rabbi: He will.

Get well card to the Rabbi in the hospital: The congregation wishes you a speedy and complete recovery by a vote of 275 to 57.

Terrorists who informed them they would be killed immediately after their last wishes were fulfilled kidnapped a Rabbi, cantor and president of the synagogue.
Rabbi: My last wish is to give a complicated and abstract very long sermon. One I always wanted to give, but was never allowed to deliver.

Cantor: My last wish is to sing a very ancient hymn, the basis of my own composition, which can last at least four hours. I have never been allowed to sing it in the synagogue.

Synagogue President: Please, please, I beg you. Shoot me now!

Child to mother: The Rabbi gave me a part in the play at Hebrew school.

Mother: Wonderful. What part is it?

Child: I play the part of a Jewish Husband.

Mother: Go back and tell the Rabbi you want a speaking role.

The Rabbi kept begging the Board of Directors to purchase a new chandelier for the synagogue.

Board President: Why are we wasting so much time talking about this? First of all, nobody here can even spell it. Secondly, we haven't got anyone who can even play it. And, lastly, what we really need is more light.

Woman to Rabbi: Thanks for giving me so many hours of your time to hear my troubles. When I came here I had a splitting headache, but now, thanks to you, it's gone.

Rabbi: Your headache is not gone, at all. Now, I have it.

Student: Rabbi, one day I hope to become a Rabbi just like you. Is there one qualification I will need above everything else?

Rabbi: Yes, imagination. You will have to imagine that somebody is paying attention to what you say.

SIGNS ON SYNAGOGUE BULLETIN BOARD

UNDER SAME MANAGEMENT FOR 5772 YEARS.

DON'T GIVE UP . . . MOSES WAS ONCE A BASKET CASE.

WHAT PART OF "THOU SHALL NOT," DON'T YOU UNDER-
STAND?

REMEMBER WHEN YOU VISIT OUR URINAL, THE FUTURE
OF THE JEWISH PEOPLE ARE IN YOUR HANDS.

ANYTIME YOU EAT PASTRAMI ON WHITE BREAD,
SOMEWHERE IN THE WORLD A JEW DIES.

ENJOY LIFE NOW, FOR ONE DAY YOU'LL BE DRIVING A
LEXUS AND EATING DINNER BEFORE 4 P.M. IN BOCA
RATON.

WHERE THERE IS SMOKE, THERE MAY BE SALMON.

ACCORDING TO JEWISH DIETARY LAWS, PORK AND
SHELLFISH MAY ONLY BE EATEN IN CHINESE
RESAURANTS.

NEVER TAKE A FRONT ROW SEAT AT A BRIS.

CHAPTER TWENTY-TWO

JEWISH HOLY DAYS

A SUMMARY OF THE major Jewish Holy Days can be put into a few words. They tried to kill us, we won, let's eat! Except, of course, on Yom Kippur.

YOM KIPPUR, THE DAY OF ATONEMENT

The Day of Atonement is the most solemn holy day in the Jewish religious calendar. Yom Kippur is the day God judges every individual according to his behavior during the past twelve months. God decrees who shall live or die during the ensuing year. Observant Jews spend the entire day in the Synagogue chanting confessional oriented prayers and asking God for favors for the coming year. It is a day of fasting, and many other deprivations, including not bathing, not having sexual intercourse not handling money, not using the phone, and not riding in a car. Modern tradition asks worshippers to pledge contributions to assist those in need.

The judging process begins ten days before, on Rosh Hashanah, the day of the Jewish New Year.

A multi millionaire businessman thanks God for doubling his wealth during the year. A man praying diverts him on his way out of the synagogue.

Man, praying: Please, Lord, help a poor sinner. Allow me to make just enough money to feed my family and maybe a new suit and shoes for my children. That's all I ask.

Businessman, smugly, whips out a roll of bills and tosses a few at the man: Don't bother God with all that little shit.

Rabbi, to worshippers playing cards on Yom Kippur: What kind of Jews do you call yourselves, playing cards on such a day as this. You are all a pack of atheists.

Player: Rabbi, with all due respect, I assure you there are no atheists in a high stake poker game.

It was Yom Kippur and the young orthodox couple were in a quandary. She was ready to go to the hospital to give birth.

Man to wife: I can only minimize Yom Kippur violations and hope God does not get too angry. I will phone for a taxi, but I will tell the expeditor he must send a non-Jewish driver.

Man and Wife listening to the expeditor on the two-way radio: Driver, have you picked up those fuckin' anti-Semites yet?

Guard at Synagogue door: Ticket, please?

Visitor: I don't have a ticket.

Guard: It's Yom Kippur. You must have a ticket.

Visitor: It's an emergency. I have to tell a friend his mother just died.

Guard: You still need a ticket.

Visitor: I promise. I'll be fast. Maybe two minutes at the most.

Guard: Okay. But, don't let me catch you praying.

Worshipper: Rabbi, I know tomorrow is Yom Kippur. But, I'm a great Jet's fan and I must watch the game on TV.

Rabbi: That's what video recorders are for.

Worshipper: You mean, I can videotape the Yom Kippur service?

Man in Synagogue on Yom Kippur: Rabbi, I know it's Yom Kippur, but I must have a drink of water. I feel faint.

Rabbi: But, it's Yom Kippur, do you realize what you're asking?

Man: I can't take it anymore. I'm dying here. Please have pity on me. Just a small drink, that's all I need.

Rabbi: Okay. Take a teaspoon of water.

Man: Thank you, Rabbi. And I promise I'll never eat pickled herring on Yom Kippur morning ever again.

PASSOVER

The Festival of Passover originated on the night of the tenth plague in Egypt. On that night every newborn Egyptian male was killed. This was an eye for an eye punishment by God commemorating Pharaoh's earlier edict to kill Hebrew newborn babies. The Israelites were required to sacrifice a lamb and smear its blood on the doorposts of their homes. The Lord would pass over their home, as he struck down the Egyptian infant males.

Throughout the ages, this became a day of remembrance celebrated as a festival to the Lord. The Jews were told what foods they could eat, how these foods could be prepared and the order of their consumption for a seven-day period. They could eat only unleavened bread, called Matzo and all traces of leavened bread were removed from their homes.

CHANUKAH

Chanukah is the Jewish Festival of Dedication. It's a memorial to their brave hero, Judas Maccabaeus. He removed the signs of pagan worship placed in the Temple by the Syrian invaders. Then, he rededicated the Synagogue for the worship of God. The Temple lamps contained just enough oil to light the candles for one night, but God intervened, and the oil lasted for eight nights. The Jewish people celebrate this miracle by lighting eight candles on a menorah, one nightly for the eight nights. Children receive presents for each night during this festival of lights. This has no connection whatsoever to the original event.

Woman to Post Office clerk: May I have 50 Chanukah stamps?
Clerk: What denomination?
Woman: God help us. Has it come to this? Give me 15 orthodox, 15 conservative and 20 reformed.

PURIM

The Book of Esther is one of the last books in the Hebrew Bible. It is the story of an unsuccessful attempt to kill the Jews living in the Persian Empire. Queen Esther, who never told the king she was Jewish, was advised by her cousin, Mordecai, that the King's life was in danger. She told the King about the plot, thus saving his life.

The King's chief assistant, Haman, who ruled as if he were king, greeted Mordecai, who had been invited to meet the King. Jealous of Mordecai, Haman asked him to bow down to him. Mordecai refused, making Haman very angry. Looking for revenge, Haman convinced the King to sign a decree ordering all the Jews to die. The King did not know Esther was Jewish until she told her husband she would be among those to die. He was furious with Haman and ordered him hanged at the same gallows Haman had prepared for Mordecai. The King now appointed Mordecai his chief assistant.

Today, Jews celebrate the Feast of Purim to remember how God delivered Esther and the Jews of the Persian Empire. Jewish families attend services where they loudly boo and shout when Haman's name is mentioned during the reading of The Book of Esther. Children often dress up in costumes to resemble the characters in the story.

CHAPTER TWENTY-THREE

JESUS CHRIST

THE TIMES

JESUS CHRIST WAS born in the Middle East over two thousand years ago. Violence and bloodshed dominated that world just as it does today. Roman legions had conquered Palestine and Jerusalem in 63BC. Rome ruthlessly suppressed an uprising 26 years later and resisting Jews died on crosses. The Jews never accepted their captors; they bore it quietly, but were indignant because of their situation. Tax collectors squeezed the impoverished people, while the Roman appointed rulers, such as Herod the Great, lived in splendor. This ancient kingdom of the Jews and the outpost of the Roman Empire was the land where Jesus would grow up.

As the Christian era dawned, revolutionaries and self proclaimed prophets abounded. Fanatic rebels called zealots spread terror. They killed the Romans as well as any people who collaborated with them.

THE BIRTH OF CHRIST

Virtually everything we know about Jesus comes from the Gospels. These first four books of the New Testament, Mathew, Mark, Luke, and John, recount his life, death and resurrection. Information about the life of Christ was spread by word of mouth for approximately thirty years after his resurrection and ascension. The young church needed a more permanent record of the things Jesus said and did. Thus, the four Gospel writers collected all the information they could and each recorded their own history of Jesus Christ, probably the most important person in the Bible.

The birth of Jesus is a well-known story. He was born to Jewish parents who were from the city of Nazareth. His father, Joseph, was a carpenter; His mother, Mary, became pregnant at fifteen years of age, while betrothed to Joseph. An integral part of Christian belief is that God endowed the Virgin Mary with her child. An angel of the Lord, who assured him of Mary's purity and the baby's divinity, visited Joseph.

Mary was in an advanced stage of pregnancy when she and Joseph had to travel to his hometown, Bethlehem, to pay the taxes due to the Roman Empire and to be counted in the census. Mary went into labor as they approached the city. There were no rooms available at the closest inn, so the couple was forced to spend the night in a cave where Jesus was born. The baby was wrapped in bands of cloth and laid in a manger. A huge bright star appeared in the Eastern Sky, and three wise men inquired about the newborn "King of the Jews" when they saw it.

When King Herod heard a ruler, who would shepherd the people of Israel, was born, he became crazed. He ordered all male infants under the age of two to be killed. Joseph and Mary were warned and fled to Egypt and didn't returned to Nazareth until Herod died.

JESUS' CHILDHOOD

Since little is known about Jesus' life until he was approximately thirty years old, it must be assumed he lived the same as any boy or man of that period. It is obvious from his parables, stories that teach a lesson, that he was a keen observer of human and environmental nature. He was raised in a strict Jewish household and was trained to be a carpenter, his father's trade.

The synagogue had a school in every town because literacy was widespread among the Jews. Jesus abandoned carpentry for study and attended a school near his home. The students concentrated on reading and writing the Scriptures and studying rabbinical decisions about questions of Jewish doctrine.

The single incident referring to his younger years is recorded in the Gospel of Luke. When Jesus was twelve years of age he made a pilgrimage to Jerusalem with his parents to celebrate Passover and to prepare for his Bar Mitzvah. At thirteen years of age, he would become an adult in the Jewish faith. Jesus went to the temple in Jerusalem and participated in lively discussions with the Rabbis, exhibiting his intelligence and maturity.

Surprisingly, there are no physical descriptions of Jesus. There are hints in the New Testament, and we can imagine he was taller than the average man, well built and handsome. He probably resembled the men of Judea, bearded and Semitic in appearance. He had an extremely charismatic personality and exuded empathy, yet was occasionally harsh and tactless. He was a man of anger as often as he was a man of understanding.

THE BAPTISM OF JESUS

When Jesus was around thirty years of age he went to hear John, "The Baptizer" speak. Jesus was so moved he asked to be baptized. John was a prophet who became famous because of his distinctive form of baptism, washing the body. His main message concerned the imminent coming of the Son of God. John's hell-fire preaching told his listeners they must repent for their sins, treat people fairly and share what they had with others. He recognized Jesus as the Messiah sent by God. Jesus then decided, to openly assume the role of God's representative on Earth.

THE MINISTRY OF JESUS

Jesus spent forty days alone in the desert praying and fasting to test his faith and to prepare himself for his future. When he returned from his self imposed trial, he became an itinerate rabbi teaching his interpretation of current religious beliefs throughout Galilee. A group, often numbering several dozens of people, accompanied him in his wanderings from village to village He attracted additional crowds along the way. However, his core of disciples consisted of twelve hand chosen men whose role was to work full time gathering people to hear Jesus. The significance of having twelve close followers recalls the twelve tribes of Israel. As the ministry increased, the disciples preached and healed and exercised other functions as well.

The most significant collections of Jesus' teachings in the Gospels occur in the Sermon on the Mount. It is here Jesus speaks as the Savior. He preached, "Blessed are the poor in spirit, for they shall be comforted. Blessed are the meek, for they shall inherit the earth. Blessed are the peacemakers, for they shall be called the children of God. Comfort for the afflicted, the impoverished, the persecuted. Mercy, charity and peace."

Everyone at the Sermon on the Mount was impressed with his presence, but very few actually listened. Thus, Jesus began to teach almost exclusively in parables. He drew striking moral and spiritual truths from short narratives about familiar subjects. These stories would form the heart of the New Testament.

Unlike the prophets of the Old Testament, Jesus openly consorted with sinners. His short ministry in Galilee spanned two to three years, and he ventured out of the province only to pay short visits to Jerusalem or to preach along the coast of Phoenicia.

JESUS, THE HEALER AND MIRACLE MAKER

Jesus is a healer who cures a large range of maladies in all four Gospels. He cured blindness, deafness, paralysis, leprosy, and mental disorders possessing evil spirits that needed exorcising. Jesus used different means to cure, mostly by touch or by word. He always responded to the cry for help by demanding a demonstration of faith by the sick person. When a healing attempt failed, the person was deemed not to have faith.

In addition to his healing powers, Jesus astonished his disciples by performing miracles, often showing his mastery over natural elements. The three most famous miracles reported in the Gospels are: walking on water, calming a storm at sea, and the story of the Loaves and the Fishes. Jesus fed thousands of people with only a small quantity of bread and fish.

Jesus walked into a homeless shelter and approached three sad looking men.
Jesus to man #1: What's troubling you, my son?
Man #1: My eyes. Every year I see less and less.
Jesus touches the man's head and his vision is restored.
Jesus to man #2: And what's troubling you, my son?
Man #2: My foot. My left foot is lame and I can hardly stand up.
Jesus touches his leg and the man leaps up on his feet. Now, Jesus approaches the third man.
Man #3, grabs a chair, fending Jesus off: Stay away from me. I'm on disability.

THE DEATH OF JESUS

Jesus' final visit to Jerusalem took place on Palm Sunday, the Sunday preceding his death on Good Friday. He arrived with his disciples for Passover, and was welcomed into the city by tremendous crowds who recognized him as a spiritual hero and a liberator of Israel from Roman rule. Jesus embarked on a breathless round of activities and ran into escalated conflicts with the Roman authorities and Rabbis over his teachings. He was predicting the fall of the Temple, criticizing the state of Roman Procurator Pontius Pilate, and insulting the Jewish Tribunal with his announcement of the arrival of God's Kingdom. Jesus was accused of breaking Jewish laws and being a threat to Roman power.

Jesus had divine knowledge of his fate and was aware his days were numbered. He asked his twelve disciples to plan a meal to celebrate Passover, the last supper he would share with them. Jesus predicted one of his disciples would betray him; Judas was bribed into betrayal.

Jesus was arrested by the Roman authorities. They were determined to prohibit his activities during the busy days of Passover. His Roman guards beat him most of the night. Jesus died on the cross the following day.

THE RESURRECTION OF JESUS

In order not to violate the laws of the Sabbath Jesus' body was hurriedly taken down from the cross on Friday at sundown, and placed in a tomb to be prepared for burial on Sunday. A close companion, Mary Magdalene, visited the tomb and found it empty. What happened to Jesus' body is the greatest mystery in the controversial story of Jesus Christ. One of the fundamental precepts of Christianity is that Jesus rose from the tomb and ascended into heaven.

Theology student to Priest: Christ died for our sins. Do we dare make his martyrdom meaningless by not committing them?

Man talking to Jesus: Jesus. I feel like no one will ever accept me.
Jesus: My attitude has always been, accept me or go to Hell.

SPREADING THE WORD

Several decades passed after the crucifixion and resurrection before the teaching of Jesus were written in the Gospels, and Christianity, as we know it, began to take shape. The books written by St. Paul contain the core of Christian teachings. He is the second most outstanding person, after Jesus Christ, in the New Testament. Although he was a devout Jew, he became the apostle to the Gentiles. Paul spread the Christian message around the world for God. He authored thirteen New Testament books. He is considered one of the great thinkers of his day and a man of practical common sense. Paul loved his own Jewish people, but spent his life bringing the Gospel to non-Jews. More than any other person, he helped Christians understand the message of salvation by faith in Jesus Christ, and preached God's expectations for Christians to live honestly and lovingly with all people.

Two other apostles are credited for spreading the words of Jesus. Peter wrote two books in the New Testament incorporating two letters. His first letter encourages Christians to have joy and trust in God even if facing persecution. He told Christians to happily await Jesus' return to earth. Since Christ suffered while he was on the cross, Christians must be prepared to suffer for him. The second letter warned about false teachers who predicted that Christ would not return a second time.

The apostle John wrote a gospel about Jesus' teachings, travel, and miracles in Judea. John tells the reader immediately that Jesus Christ is the Son of God, and includes many details of Jesus' life not recorded earlier.

Man to friend: I was stopped in traffic and read a bumper sticker that said, "Need help. Call Jesus. 1 800 914 8343." I called, out of curiosity.
Friend: So, what happened?
Man: A Mexican showed up with a lawnmower.

The line of cars followed each other as they rolled out of the Church parking lot after services. A parishioner waiting for a red light read a bumper sticker on the car in front of him. "HONK IF YOU LOVE JESUS." He honked.

The man in the front car rolled down his window and screamed back: Can't you see the freaking light is red, you fuckin' moron.

CHAPTER TWENTY-FOUR

THE NEW TESTAMENT

R ELIGIOUS LEADERS IN Israel realized the destruction of Israel was imminent at the start of the Jewish-Roman war in 66BC. The Jewish nation was decimated and scattered by the Roman armies. It is estimated over one million Jews died in the region, including large populations in Egypt and Syria. The disaster motivated Jewish leaders to salvage their belief in God by creating new Scripture, now known, as the New Testament. It became apparent God would live through the teachings of Jesus and his apostle, Paul. The Gospels written by Jewish holy men, Mathew, Mark, Luke and John, believed if one believed in Jesus he could be saved from sin and achieve unity with God. These Gospels provided the groundwork for Christianity.

The New Testament doesn't offer a new doctrine of God, but simply proclaims the Old Testament God has taken definitive action. The God of Abraham, Isaac, and Jacob is now the God of Jesus Christ, the awaited Messiah. The core of the New Testament focuses upon the death and resurrection of Jesus as well as his short ministry. The premise that Jesus would return provided new hope for Israel's belief in a new heaven and a new earth.

The word "testament" in the Bible refers to an unbreakable agreement or covenant between God and his people. In the Old Testament God made a covenant with the Israelites at Mount Sinai and repeated it several other times. He promised if the people would obey him by following his commands, He would insure their well-being.

The word "testament" also refers to the unbreakable written instructions, a will, left when one dies. The apostle Paul compared God's covenant with Israel to a will used in Greece. This document cannot be changed. Paul showed that Christ's coming did not destroy the Old Testament covenant, but fulfilled it.

THE WILL

To my wife, I leave half my assets.
To my son, I leave all of my businesses.
To my daughter: I leave the other half of my assets.
To my Partner, who told me health was better than wealth, I leave my sun lamp.
To my brother in law, who I promised to mention in my will, "Hi, Sid."

Woman at gravesite: Darling, it's been two long years since you left me.
Passerby: Who are you mourning?
Woman: My husband. I miss him so much.
Passerby: Your husband? It says, "In memory of Rosie Glutton" on the tombstone.
Woman: Oh, yes! It's the WILL. He put everything in my name!

CHAPTER TWENTY-FIVE

ST. PETER HOLDS THE KEYS TO HEAVEN

ST PETER TO a young man: Have you done any good deeds?

Young Man: Oh, yes, I have. I saved a young lady from being attacked by a tough gang of bikers. I was driving down the highway and saw a group of about fifty bikers assaulting a poor girl. I stopped, got out of my car, grabbed a tire iron from my trunk, and approached the gang leader. He was huge. He wore a studded leather jacket and was wrapped in a chain from his neck to his belt. I grabbed him by his balls with my left hand and hit him over his head with the tire iron in my right hand. I yelled to the others that they better leave the young girl go, or I'll do to each of you what I just did your leader. I told them they were sick deranged animals and to get on their bikes before I counted to ten.

St. Peter: Really? This incident doesn't appear in our records. When did all this take place?

Young Man: About two minutes ago.

Woman at Pearly Gates: Could I be reunited with my dear husband who died twenty years ago?

St. Peter: What's his name?

Woman: John Smith.

St. Peter: That's a very common name, sometimes hard to locate. However, we can identify people by their last words. Do you remember what they were?

Woman. Sure. He said if I ever slept with another man after he was gone he would turn over in his grave.

St. Peter: Oh, you mean spinning John Smith.

A large group of people found themselves at the Pearly Gates to Heaven. St. Peter had to make decisions about who deserved entry.

St. Peter: The line to my left are for those men dominated by their women on earth. The line on my right is for men who dominated their woman.

The line on the left became two miles long. The line on the right that dominated their woman had only one man standing there.

God appeared at the Pearly Gates: You men should be ashamed of yourselves. I created you in my image to take charge. Yet, your partners dominated you all. There is only one man who stood up for his rights and made me proud. Learn from him. Tell them, my son, how did you manage to be the only one on that line.

Only man: I don't know. To tell the truth, my wife told me to stand here.

Fifty brothers died in an earthquake at the monastery and went to heaven at the same time.

St. Peter: We will do the entry test together at these Pearly Gates. First of all, how many of you played around with little boys?

Forty-nine hands went up.

St. Peter: You forty-nine can go down to hell and take the deaf bastard with you.

St. Peter, talking to three nurses: Before I admit any of you I must see if you are eligible.

Nurse #1: I'm an emergency nurse and I've saved thousands of lives.

St. Peter: Okay, come in.

Nurse #2: I'm a visiting nurse and also saved thousands of lives.

St. Peter: Okay, come in.

Nurse #3: I was a managed health care nurse and saved the insurance companies thousands of dollars.

St. Peter: Okay, come in, but you can only stay for three days.

St. Peter was manning the Pearly Gates when fifty New Yorkers arrived. It was the first time St. Peter ever met New Yorkers. (Just Kidding!)

St. Peter to God: I've got 50 people from New York at the gate. Is it okay to let them in?

God: We don't want Heaven overrun with New Yorkers. It's safe to admit ten of the most virtuous, if you're lucky enough to find ten.

St. Peter returned to the group to relay the message, but returned to God immediately in a state of panic.

God: What happened?

St. Peter: They're gone.

God: What? All the New Yorkers are gone?

St. Peter: No, the Pearly Gates!

Here are the top ten reasons St. Peter was leery of New Yorkers.

10: Their front doors have more than three locks on them.

9: The most frequently used part of the car is the horn.

8: They all suffer from middle finger arthritis.

7: They go to hockey games just for the fighting.

6: They consider eye contact to be an overt act of aggression.

5: They believe swearing at people in their language makes them multi-lingual.

4: They have never visited the Empire State Building or the Statue of Liberty.

3: When Chinese New Year firecrackers explode, mothers calm their children by telling them, "It's only gunfire."

2: They say, "city", and expect the world to know they mean Manhattan.

1: They think Central Park is nature.

New York Judge: Tell me exactly what happened.
Defendant: I was in the city library and there was a book I wanted to borrow. I waited in line for over an hour when I finally reached the clerk at the desk. She told me my library card had expired. So, I filled out the forms for another card and was sent to another long line. I waited on this line for another hour, although it felt like eternity. When I was finally at the desk, this wise-ass asked me to prove I was from New York City. So, I stabbed him.

A very apprehensive tourist visiting New York for the very first time approached a typical New Yorker.
Tourist: I beg your pardon, sir, can you tell me the correct way to the Empire State Building, or should I just go fuck myself?

Anytime four New Yorkers get into a taxi without arguing, a bank robbery has just taken place.

CHAPTER TWENTY-SIX

KEEPERS OF THE CHURCH

IN THE NEW Testament, "The Church" signifies a group of believers in Jesus Christ who assemble together. Every local church is part of the Universal Church and is headed by Jesus Christ. Not unlike the synagogue, the Church building is used for assembly, prayers, ceremonies, and celebrations.

There are dozens of Christian religious groups differing from each other in doctrine, practice, organization, authority, ethics, and the like. However, they all have a common foundation stemming from the teachings of Jesus Christ, the Son of God. The Roman Catholic Church is the largest Church in the world.

THE POPE

The Roman Catholic Church named the apostle Peter as founder of the Church of Rome and the first Pope. He was Pope for about twenty-five years and was ultimately canonized as a Saint. The Pope is the Supreme Pontiff of the Universal Church and Vicar to Jesus

Christ. Their main responsibility is to maintain the Church's Doctrines of Faith and Morals.

Members of the Sacred College of Cardinals are chosen by the Pope to be his chief assistants and advisors in the administration of the Church. One of their duties is to elect the new Pope when the current Pope dies. The Council of Bishops, under the Cardinals in the hierarchy of the Church, advises on matters of doctrine and policy.

Pope to Cardinals: I have some really good news and some really bad news. Here is the good news. I got a call from God this morning. Jesus Christ has returned to our world.
Cardinal: What in Heaven's name could possibly be bad news?
Pope: The bad news is She was calling from Salt Lake City.

A man found himself on a plane seated next to the Pope. He sat quietly, not wanting to disturb the Pope, who was doing a crossword puzzle.
Pope: Excuse me, sir? Do you know a four letter word referring to a woman that ends in, "UNT?"
Man, thinking to himself, decides he can't give the Pope the vulgar word that leaped to his mind. Ah, he thinks. I've got it.
Man: Your Holiness, I think you're looking for the word, "aunt."
Pope: Of course. Do you have an eraser?

Visitor to Pope: Your Holiness, have you heard this joke about two Polaks who . . . .
Pope: Stop there. Don't you know I'm Polish?
Visitor: That's okay. I'll tell it slowly.

Priest to God: Will priests ever be allowed to marry?
God: Not in your lifetime.
Priest: Will we ever have female priests?
God: Not in your lifetime.
Priest: Will there ever be another German Pope?
God: Not in my lifetime.

The Cardinal advised the Pope his test results indicated he potentially had a fatal testicular disease. The best chances for a cure was sex with a woman.

Pope: I agree, reluctantly. There are four conditions.

Cardinal: What are they, Holy Father?

Pope: First, the woman has to be blind so she can't see who I am. Second, she has to be deaf so she does not recognize my voice. Third, she must be dumb so she can't tell the world.

Cardinal: Father, I have just the woman for you. Leave it all to me. Wait a minute. You said four conditions. What's the fourth?

Pope: Big Tits.

The President of the Kosher Meat Association had an audience with the Pope.

President: Holy Father, I am prepared to donate one million dollars to the church to change the words of the Lord's Prayer to, "give us this day our daily salami."

Pope: That's preposterous.

President: Ten million.

Pope turns to his secretary: When does our contract with Pillsbury expire?

PRIESTS

A Priest has authority to perform sacred rites and advise the parishioners about personal matters. Priests take a vow of abstinence, remain celibate, and never marry. They are expected to live a simple life with a minimum of worldly goods. The School of Priests was first established in the second century.

The Church Priests usually hear the confessions of the parishioners. These are oral admissions of sins they have committed that the Priests pass on to God. This ritual is done in secrecy and often calls for penance in seeking absolution.

Confessor: Oh, Father, I have sinned. I am having an affair with four different women all over town.
Priest: How can you do such a thing?
Confessor: I've got a moped.

Aging Jewish Man: Father, last night I met this beautiful young girl and had an unbelievable time. She did things to me I never dreamt could be done. Listen, first she . . . .
Priest: Hold on there. Why are you telling me all this? Aren't you Jewish?
Man: Telling you! I'm telling everyone.

Nun: Father, I seek absolution for my sins. I never wear under panties under my habit.
Priest: That's not so bad, Sister. Just say five Hail Mary's and then do five cartwheels.

Priest in training hearing confession: What is your sin, my Son?
Parishioner: Father, I have committed sodomy.
Priest: Let me check with an alter boy to learn the accurate penance for this sin.
Priest to Alter boy: What does father O'Neil usually give for sodomy?
Alter Boy: A chocolate ice cream cone and a coke.

Parishioner: Father, bless me for I have sinned. I have been with a loose woman.
Priest: Is that you Johnny?
Johnny: Yes, Father. It is I.
Priest: Who was the woman you were with?
Johnny: I cannot tell you, Father, for I don't want to ruin her reputation.
Priest: Was it Mary?
Johnny: No, Father.
Priest: Was it Melinda?
Johnny: No, Father.
Priest: Was it Suzie?

Johnny: No, Father.

Priest: Very well. Say five Our Fathers and three Hail Mary's.

Friend to Johnny: What Happened?

Johnny: I got five Our Fathers and three Hail Mary's, and three good leads.

Young girl to Priest: Bless me, Father, for I have sinned. Last night my boyfriend made love to me five times.

Priest: You must go home and suck the juice out of six lemons.

Girl: Will that absolve me?

Priest: No, but it will wipe that smug look off your face.

State Trooper to Priest: Have you been drinking?

Priest: Just water, officer.

Trooper: Then why do I smell wine?

Priest: Good Lord. Jesus has done it again!

Parishioner: I've lived 70 years already. Over the years I've often prayed for some things very hard and nothing happens.

Priest: He does not answer right away, and often your needs change. Yet, all of a sudden, you can wake up one day and find a Barbie Doll on your dresser.

CONFESSIONS OUTSIDE THE CHURCH

Man: Honey, you must know something before we get married. I'm a fanatic golfer. I eat, sleep, and drink golf. Golf is my whole life. Just understand, you're marrying a golf addict.

Woman: I can live with that. Now, I'll tell you my secret. I'm a hooker.

Man: A hooker. I can live with that. Listen, next time, keep your head down, your left arm straight, and then swing through the ball.

THE PRIEST AND HIS FLOCK

Woman to Priest: Oh, Father. I've got terrible news.
Priest: What is it, Mary?
Mary: My husband passed away last night.
Priest: That's very sad news. Did he have any last request?
Mary: Yes, he did, Father.
Priest: What did he say?
Mary: He said, "Please, please, Mary, I beg you. Put down that gun."

Boy to Priest: Oh, Father, I've got terrible news.
Priest: What is it, my son?
Boy: My mother passed away last night and she was only 57 years old.
Priest: That's sad news to me as well. I know she was a good Catholic woman and had eight children with her first husband.
Boy: I am the last child of seven more she had with her second husband.
Priest: At last they are finally together.
Boy: Father, do you mean mom and her first husband, or mom and my father?
Priest: Neither. I mean her legs.

A Priest sat down on a train next to a drunk reading a newspaper.
Drunk: Say, Father, what causes arthritis?
Priest: My son, it's caused by loose living, hanging out with cheap women, homelessness, too much alcohol, and a complete contempt for your fellow man.
Drunk: Well, I'll be dammed.
Priest: I'm sorry. I didn't mean to come on so strong. How long have you had arthritis?
Drunk: I don't have arthritis, Father. I was just reading here that the Pope does.

Priest to Parishioner: How have you managed to stay married to the same woman for almost 50 years?

Parishioner: I've tried to treat her nicely. I spent money on her. Best of all, I took her to Italy for our twenty-fifth anniversary.

Priest: So, what are you planning for your fiftieth anniversary?

Parishioner: I'm going to go and get her.

Priest to patient in hospital bed: I'm here to give you the last rites. Are you motioning for a paper and pencil to write something?

The patient scribbles a note and dies. The Priest pockets the note.

Priest, at funeral: Ladies and Gentleman, I find I am wearing the same jacket I wore when I gave Joe the last rites. I just found the note he wrote. It was his last message and I'm sure it's something wonderful. I'm going to ask Joe's wife to read it aloud.

Joe's Wife: Get off my fucking oxygen tube.

Parishioner: Father, something terrible is happening. My wife is poisoning me.

Priest: How can that be?

Parishioner: I'm positive, Father. What should I do?

Priest: Let me talk to her and see what I can find out. I'll let you know.

Priest, next day: I spoke to your wife for more than four hours on the phone. Do you want my advice?

Parishioner: Sure.

Priest: Take the poison.

Priest to Bride at Italian Wedding: Do you take Franco, Giuseppe, Antonio, and Leonardo to be your husband?

Bride: Father, there must be some mistake. I'm only marrying Frank. Sometimes, I call him Frankie when we're in bed.

Two beggars sit side by side on a street in Rome. One wears a Cross-, the other a Star of David.

Passing Priest: I notice the people only put money into the hat of the man wearing the Cross.

Star of David beggar: So, what's the problem?

Passing Priest: My poor fellow, don't you understand? This is a Catholic country. People aren't going to give you money if you sit there wearing the Star of David. People will purposely give money to the beggar wearing the Cross, simply out of spite.

Star of David beggar whispers to beggar wearing the Cross: Look who's trying to teach the Cohen Brothers about marketing.

Priest: What should we do before we can expect forgiveness of sin?

Parishioner in front row: Sin!

NUNS

Nuns are women who belong to a religious order and take solemn vows of poverty, chastity, and obedience. Their lives are spent serving Jesus Christ by teaching and helping unfortunates.

Nun to Pub patron: You should be ashamed of yourself, sitting outside this pub and drinking alcohol. Alcohol is the blood of the devil.

Patron: How do you know that?

Nun: Mother Superior told me.

Patron: Have you ever had a drink yourself?

Nun: Ridiculous! Of course not.

Patron: Then let me buy you a drink. If you still believe afterwards that it is evil, I'll give up drinking.

Nun: How could I, a Nun, sit outside this public pub and be seen drinking?

Patron: I'll ask the barman to put your drink in a teacup.

Nun: Well, then, I'll reluctantly agree.

Patron to Barman: Another shot for me and a triple vodka on the rocks. Can you put the vodka in a teacup?

Barman: Oh, No! For cryin' out loud, it's not that nun again, is it?

Nun #1: I found pornographic magazines when I was cleaning the Father's room and threw them into the trash.

Nun #2: I found a pack of condoms in the room, as well.

Nun #1: So, what did you do with them?

Nun #2: I poked them full of holes with a needle.

Nun #1: Oh, SHIT!

An old Jewish man was in a Catholic hospital awaiting an operation.
Nun: Who will be responsible for your bill?
Man: Well, my only living relative is my sister. She's an old maid and
    converted to Catholicism and became a nun.
Nun: Just a minute! We are not old maids. We are married to Jesus
    Christ.
Man: Fine, then send the bill to my brother-in-law.

THE PROTESTANTS

Ministers, reverends, clergymen and others are the keepers of the
Protestant religion. They lead their church and offer advise, comfort,
aid and services to their followers. These leaders are not subject to
the celibacy rules of the Catholic Church. Protestantism was founded
centuries after ancient Biblical times.

Man to Born Again Missionary: I'm a little indignant when I'm told
    I'm going to Hell if I haven't been born again. Pardon me for
    getting it right the first time!

A Minister is seated next to a redneck on a flight across the country.
Redneck to Attendant: I'll have a whiskey and soda.
Attendant to Minister: And you, sir?
Minister: I'd rather be savagely raped by a band of brazen whores
    than let a drop of liquor touch these lips.
Redneck: Cancel my drink. I didn't think we had a choice.

CHAPTER TWENTY-SEVEN

CONVERSION

CONVERSION REFERS TO the change of allegiance from one religion or a branch of one religion to another. In certain Biblical episodes, conversions were calls by God for an individual to play new roles. The stories of God's encounters with Abraham, Jacob and Moses reflect transfers of tribal allegiances to a new deity.

In the New Testament there is evidence of people changing from other religions to Judaism, just as some subsequently moved to Christianity. The most dramatic is Paul, who was struck with a bright light as he was going to persecute Christians. All the Disciples slowly learned what it meant to convert to Christ.

Jewish convert to friend: In some ways I still feel Jewish, even though I now eat pastrami on white bread. I go to church every Sunday. I exchange Christmas gifts with all my friends. But, I'm still afraid of dogs.

Two Jewish friends notice a big sign at the front door of a church. CONVERT TO CATHOLICISM AND GET $20.00

Jewish friend #1: I'm thinking of doing it.

Jewish friend #2: Are you crazy?

Jewish friend #1: No, I'm not. And, in fact, I'm going to do it.

He enters the church and comes out twenty minutes later.

Jewish friend #2: So, did you get the $20.00?

Converted friend #1: Is that all you people think about?

Convert #1: To be honest with you, I did not convert from Judaism to Christianity for any strong convictions. My Christian wife insisted upon it.

Convert #2: To be honest with you, I converted from Judaism to Christianity in order to rise in the legal system. My appointment as a Federal Judge may have something to do with my new religion.

Convert #3: I converted because I think the teachings of Christianity are superior to those of Judaism.

Convert #1, spitting out his coffee: What do you take us for, a couple of goys?

Atheist to Rabbi: I have seen the light, Rabbi. From now on I'll attend synagogue services regularly, I promise.

Rabbi: Remember, going to the synagogue doesn't make you a Jew any more than going to a poultry farm makes you a chicken.

Priest to Converter: Remember, you are now forbidden to eat meat on Fridays.

Priest, at unannounced visit to converter's home: Just as I suspected, you are eating a huge steak.

Converter: Meat? This is a salmon steak.

Priest: I'm not a fool. How can anyone make fish out of meat?

Converter: The same way you make a Catholic out of a Jew. I sprinkled water on it,

CHAPTER TWENTY-EIGHT

CHRISTIAN HOLY DAYS

CHRISTMAS

CHRISTMAS IS CELEBRA-TED on December 25th as a church festival to commemorate the birth of Jesus Christ. There are questions about the date and the actual year of his birth. The Gospel of Mathew says Jesus was born in the last two years of the reign of King Herod, which places his birth around 4 B.C. The more widely accepted version in Luke places his birth around 6 or 7 B.C. Corroborating this approximate date is the famous 17th century astronomer, Keller. He proved that in the year 7 B.C. Jupiter and Saturn would have been aligned so as to appear as an unfamiliar and extremely bright star in the sky, perhaps appearing as the Star of Bethlehem followed by the Three Wise Men.

Airline Pilot: We have landed in Israel. Please remain seated with your seat belt fastened until the plane is at a complete stop and the seat belt sign is turned off. To those of you now standing in the aisle, we wish you a Happy Chanukah. To those who have remained in their seats, we wish you a Merry Christmas.

The worst thing about being Jewish at Christmas time is standing in line at the post office because the lines are so long. They should have a Jewish express line.

Man, pushing to the front of the post office line: Look, I'm Jewish. It's not a gift. I'm just mailing my proxy vote to my broker.

CHRISTMAS VERSUS CHANUKAH

* Christmas is one day, the same day, every year . . . December 25th. Jews love Christmas, as it's another paid holiday. They usually eat Christmas dinner at a Chinese restaurant. The eight days of Chanukah occur around Christmas, but the dates vary from year to year. Jews are never certain when Chanukah begins, forcing them to consult a calendar every Christmas season.

* There is only one way to spell Christmas. No one knows exactly how to spell Chanukah, or Hannukah, or even Chanuka.

* Christmas celebrants end up with staggering electric bills. Since Jews use candles they are spared inflated bills.

* Christian homes smell great with the aromas of freshly baked cookies and cakes. Homes preparing for Chanukah smell of frying oil, potatoes, and onions for potato pancakes. (Latkes.)

* Christmas has wonderful songs: WHITE CHRISTMAS, WE WISH YOU A MERRY CHRISTMAS, JINGLE BELLS, WINTER WONDERL AND, AND FROSTY THE SNOWMAN. Chanukah has, DREIDEL, DREIDEL, DREIDEL.

* Christmas has a common greeting . . . Merry Christmas. Chanukah has a common greeting . . . Merry Christmas.

* Christmas has lots of decorations . . . wreaths, mistletoe, tinsel, glass ornaments, hanging stocking, and multi colored lights. Chanukah has a menorah.

* Christmas has a fireplace, a focal point to share holiday warmth, and to welcome Santa Clause and a mantle for holiday photos. Chanukah has a dad who's still learning how to use the fireplace.

Lady on phone to army chaplain: I am giving a Christmas party in my home on Friday and would like to invite several soldiers from the fort. Just one request, please do not send any men of the Jewish faith.

Doorbell rings on Friday and 4 black soldiers appear: Merry Christmas, Ma'am. Captain Cohen done sent us.

EASTER

Easter is the day Christians celebrate Christ's resurrection. However, the New Testament makes no mention of this celebration. Early on, after Christ's death, Jewish Christians celebrated his resurrection on Passover, while Gentile Christians celebrated on an unknown Sunday. In 300 A.D. an exact Sunday was set. It is the first Sunday after the full moon in the spring, falling late March through April. Just an aside, the Easter Bunny and Easter Eggs have nothing to do with the real meaning of Easter.

CHAPTER TWENTY-NINE

PRIEST, MINISTER, AND RABBI

A Priest, Minister and a Rabbi walk into a bar.
Bartender: Hey, this is not a joke. Is it?

YES, IT IS a joke, and here are many more in the category of religious humor.

At an interfaith conference a priest, a minister and a rabbi were asked, "What would you like people to say about you after you die?"
Priest: I hope people will say I was able to rise above the scandals plaguing the Catholic Church at this time. I hope people will say I was a caring and thoughtful messenger of God.
Minister: When I die, I hope people will say I saved hundreds of souls by bringing them to Christ. I hope people will say I was able to shepherd my flock through crisis.
Rabbi, without pausing to think: I hope people will say, "Look, he's breathing."

Priest: I must own up to a terrible impulse to drink.

Minister: I don't have trouble with liquor, but I must own up to a terrible impulse towards women.
Rabbi: I am also troubled by sin. I have this terrible impulse to gossip.

JUST THE RABBI AND PRIEST

A Rabbi is driving a Priest to an Interfaith meeting. The car hits speeds of ninety miles an hour. The Rabbi loses control and skids into the woods demolishing the car. Yet, they are both unhurt and leave the car.
Rabbi: This is a sign from God recognizing our belief in Him. Look, the bottle of wine is also intact. Let's celebrate these miracles. Here, take a few swigs.
Priest: Oh, my. I drank half a bottle. Here, take some.
Rabbi, corking the bottle: No, thanks.
Priest: Aren't you having any wine?
Rabbi: No. I think I'll just wait for the police.

Rabbi to Priest: Have you ever been with a woman?
Priest: I must confess. Yes, I was with a woman before I entered the Priesthood. So, Rabbi, have you ever tasted ham?
Rabbi: Yes. I tasted ham when I was a young man. Wouldn't you say a woman is better?

Rabbi, attending a prize fight with a Priest: I see the fighter crossing himself. What does that mean??
Priest: Not a damn thing, if he can't fight.

Priest to Rabbi: Talking about the joy of giving, what would you do if you had two cars?
Rabbi: I'd give you one, of course.
Priest: What would you do if you had two houses?
Rabbi: I'd give you one, of course.
Priest: What would you do if you had two chickens?
Rabbi: That's not fair. You know I have two chickens.

IT DOESN'T HAVE TO BE A PRIEST, A MINISTER AND RABBI ALL THE TIME

A Black, a Jew, and a Redneck are praying together to God.

Black: I'd like my own country where the brothers and sisters can live in peace and harmony in freedom, forever.

Jew: I'd like my own country where Jews can live in peace and harmony with no threats from neighbors and pursue a happy life forever.

God: Done, your prayers are answered.

Redneck: Now, God, let me get this straight. The Blacks are all going to live in their own country? The Jews are all going to live in their own country?

God: That's correct. So, what's your wish?

Redneck: Okay, then. Fuck it. I'll just take a diet Coke.

CHAPTER THIRTY

MEDICINE AND THE BIBLE

IT IS GENERALLY agreed that modern medicine originates from Greek Hippocratic traditions. However, Western medicine is based on the former as well as respect for the patient. This element introduced morality into the practice of medicine. Man's obligation to care for others originated in the Bible, but was included later in modern medicine.

People in Biblical times lacked proper understanding of the causes and progression of disease. There was a tendency to see sickness as the result of divine punishment for wrongdoing. It was God alone who sent disease and disaster. God also gave good health and well being. The Bible infrequently mentions physicians, but healers are cited. However, consulting a healer denied the primary role of God, lack of faith in Him, and an unwillingness to acknowledge personal sin.

Religion and medicine are bound together in The Old Testament. Ancient Israel's legal codes did not separate physical disease from ritual purity. The sanitary codes contained important regulations to promote good health and to prevent the spread of epidemic diseases in the community. In the New Testament, medical treatment entailed fasting and praying, and the Bible did not influence positive medical care.

The knowledge of medicine remained in its infancy until the great philosopher, physician and Rabbi, Maimonides was born in the 14th Century. He became the ablest practitioner of his time, creating the beginning of modern medicine. His lingering doubts about creation led him to believe that sin and punishment were not the causes of illness. He believed Man needed to learn about the causes and effects of disease. He began writing and reevaluating century old snippets and ideas from Hippocrates and others. He developed his own theories in new areas such as diet, sexual hygiene, impotence, poisons, asthma, hemorrhoids and hypochondria. As a practicing physician in the Royal Court of Egypt, he organized the first known glossary of drugs. He warned against overeating and believed wine was healthful in moderation. He recommended philosophy for calm mental health.

Medicine and theology became increasingly divorced from one another after the time of Maimonides. Scientific principles and new pure knowledge allowed medicine to develop. However, a healing ministry, biblically based, still exists in Christianity. Exorcism, or the conjuring up of evil spirits practiced by the Catholic clergy, supposedly heals and improves the well being of believers. Healing by touch, practiced by Christian Evangelists, cures illness immediately.

There is no end to exhausting "doctor stories." Here's a dose of their own medicine. There are family doctors, nose doctors, throat doctors, ear doctors, gynecologists and many more. Any place you have a hole, a doctor can create a career. If they can't help you, they will send you to a surgeon. Why? So he can make a new hole! Speaking of holes, there are also proctologists. Some use two fingers in case the patient wants a second opinion.

THE ART OF MISCOMMUNICATION

Old man: Right, doc. I insist on being castrated.
Doctor: You're not serious?

Old man: I sure am. If you won't do it, I'll find a doctor who will.

Doctor: Okay, then. Lie down on the table.

The old man's operation was successful. As he was coming out of anesthesia, the doctor spoke to him.

Doctor: You know, while I was getting you ready I should have asked if you wanted to be circumcised, first.

Old man: For God's sake. That was the damn word I was looking for.

Unfortunately, the wires got crossed, and the man who went to the hospital for a circumcision received a sex change operation instead.

Doctor: I must apologize. There has been an error. I cut off your penis and replaced it with a vagina.

Patient: You mean I'll never experience an erection again?

Doctor: Well, you will, but it will be somebody else's.

The patient and his wife are receiving directions from the doctor.

Doctor: Take this box of suppositories and take two a day, rectally.

Patient to wife, as they are leaving: What's rectally?

Wife: Who knows? It's just fancy doctor language. Just take it like your other medications. Swallow them with a cup of tea.

The patient returned to the doctor's office a week later, without relief.

Doctor: I don't understand? Did you take two a day rectally, as I prescribed?

Patient: Rectally, shmecterly, for all the good they did, I might just as well have shoved them up my ass.

The doctor told his elderly patient suffering from stomach problems to drink water with Epsom salts one hour before breakfast. At the end of the week the patient returned and told the doctor he was feeling worse.

Doctor: Really? Did you drink the warm salt water an hour before breakfast each day?

Patient: No. I could only do about ten minutes.

A woman received medication for her elderly husband.

Doctor: Give him the pills on Sunday, Wednesday, and Friday. He should skip the rest of the days of the week.

A month later the wife returns and reports that her husband died of a heart attack.

Doctor: It's hard to understand, he didn't have heart problems. I hope it wasn't a side effect of the medication.

Wife: Oh, no. The pills did him good. It was the skipping that killed him.

Doctor: What seems to be the problem?

Woman: I'm suffering from a discharge.

Doctor: Please undress and lie down on the examination table.

The doctor put on his rubber glove and began investigating her private parts.

Doctor: How does that feel?

Woman: Absolutely wonderful! But the discharge is coming from my ear.

The patient is lying in the hospital bed with an oxygen mask over his face.

Patient, mumbling behind his mask: Nurse, are my testicles black?

Nurse # 1: I don't know, I'm here to sponge you.

Patient: Nurse, are my testicles black?

Nurse #2: I can't tell. I'm only here to sponge you.

Patient: Call the head nurse.

Head Nurse: What's the problem?

Patient: Are my testicles black?

Head nurse, whips down the blankets, pulls down his pajamas, moves his penis out of the way, and takes a good look: There's nothing wrong with your testicles.

Patient, whisks off his oxygen mask: Are my test results back?

Man to friend: The doctor ran a bunch of tests for the pain in my back. He gave me some pills, asked me to stay in bed for a week, and told me to sit down whenever I have to pee. Can you imagine that? A grown man having to sit and pee?

Friend: Why did he tell you that?

Man: Well, with my bad back and all, I guess he doesn't want me to pick up anything too heavy.

Woman: Doc, I'm concerned about those hormones you gave me for my rare skin ailment. I've started growing hair in places I've never grown hair before.

Doctor: A little hair growth is a perfectly normal side effect of testosterone. Just where has this hair appeared?

Woman: On my balls!

A young medical student approached the patient brandishing a syringe.

Student: Nothing to worry about . . . just a little prick with a needle.

Patient: Yes, I know who you are, but what are you going to do?

A man went to a woman doctor. She told him to take off all his clothing in the examining room. After a few moments there was a knock on the door. The doctor entered and examined him closely.

Doctor: Do you have any questions?

Man: Just one. Why did you knock?

Wife: The doctor said he had never seen such a perfect body.

Husband: What did he say about your fat ass?

Wife: Funny thing, he didn't mention you at all.

A beautiful girl is laying on a gurney waiting to go into the operating room. A young man in a white coat lifts the girl's sheet to examine her body. He calls over his colleague, another young man in a white coat They have a brief discussion, and he also examines her. A third man arrives, ready to enter the operating room. He stops, lifts the sheet and also examines her.

Girl: Are these examinations absolutely necessary?

Man: I have no idea. We're here to paint the ceiling.

Patient: I have an appointment with Dr. Jones.

Receptionist: Dr. Jones has been called away on an emergency. Dr. Fzzbzstczywwx can see you.
Patient: Which doctor?
Receptionist: Not at all. He's highly qualified.

Patient: Doc, everywhere I touch with my finger hurts.
Doctor: Show me. Touch your nose.
Patient: Hurts.
Doctor: Your elbow.
Patient: Hurts
Doctor: Your neck.
Patient: Hurts.
Doctor: Get undressed. You need a complete and thorough examination.
Patient: Now that you're finished Doc, what's the problem?
Doctor: You have a broken finger.

She was in her eighties, healthy as a horse, and had never been examined by a gynecologist before. She was silent, but wide eyed during the examination.
Lady: You seem like such a nice young man. Tell me, does your mother know what you do for a living?

ADVICE

Patient: I'm confused, doc. Tuesday, you said eat red meat. Wednesday, you said no red meat. Yesterday good, today bad. What's going on?
Doctor: Listen, you'd be surprised how medicine has progressed in the last twenty-four hours.

Doctor to paunchy patient: Take this bottle of pills, but don't swallow any. Just spill them on the floor three times a day and pick them up one at a time.

Patient: Please, don't tell me that I'm overweight.

Doctor: Okay. According to my height and weight chart you are four inches too short.

Doctor: The best thing for you to do is cut out all sweets and fatty foods, give up alcohol, and stop smoking.
Patient: To be honest, doc, I don't deserve the best. What's the second best?

Doctor: My examination indicates a serious heart murmur. Do you have a sex life?
Patient: Of course!
Doctor: I'm afraid at your age you'll have to give up half your sex life if you want your heart to last.
Patient: Which half should I give up, the looking or the thinking?

Man to friend: My doctor is always sending me to other doctors, I don't know if he's really a doctor or if he's a booking agent.

Old Man: Doctor, I met this beautiful young girl who wants to have sex. She told me she had either VD or TB. I just can't remember which.
Doctor: If she coughs, fuck her.

Man who stutters: I have this st-st-stuttering problem. I-I was wo-wo-wondering if you c-c-c-could help me?
Doctor: Take off your clothes and let me check you over.
Man: Okay, doc.
Doctor: I see your problem. Your penis is so big it's pulling on your abdominal muscles and that is causing a strain on your vocal cords. I've got to cut nine inches off to help you.
Man: Go a-a-ahead, d-d-doc. I c-c-can't take anymore. Just d-d-do it.
Six months later, the man who stuttered, returned to the doctor's office.
Man: I must say, doc, the operation was a complete success, but my sex life really sucks now. I would like the operation reversed. Please put back what you took off.

Doctor: F-f-f-fuck you!

A doctor giving a lecture on health and well being tells his audience, "It's best to begin the day with five minutes of light exercise followed by five minutes of deep breathing. Then, take a short hot shower and feel rosy all over, all day long."
Voice from the audience: Cut to the chase, doc. Tell us more about Rosie.

Nurse: Doctor, your last patient, the one you just gave a clean bill of health, dropped dead as he was leaving the office.
Doctor: Turn him around. Make it look like he was just walking in.

Doctor to medical student: As you can see from the x-rays, the patient limps because his fibula and tibia are radically arched. What would you do in a case like this?
Student, pondering: Well, I suppose I would limp as well.

A veterinarian visits her M.D.
Veterinarian: Hey, Doc. I'm a vet. I don't need to ask my patients all those kinds of questions. I can tell what's wrong just by looking at them. Why can't you?
Doctor, as he writes her a prescription: Here you are. Of course, if this doesn't work, I'll have to put you down.

Ninety-year old man: Doc, I just met this young girl who wants to have sex with me. Give me an injection or something,
Doctor: There's no such thing, and besides, you're too old.
Old man: But, doc, my friend is also ninety years old and says he has sex ten times a week.
Doctor: Okay, so you say it also.

Patient: My penis has developed small holes. It sprays in all directions when I pee.
Doctor: Here, take this card. The name and address are on it.
Patient: Is this the name of a specialist?

Doctor: No. It's the name of a clarinet teacher. He'll teach you how to hold it.

Doctor: You have a combination of herpes, aids, gonorrhea and syphilis. The only cure is complete isolation and a diet of pancakes.
Patient: Why pancakes?
Doctor: It's the only food we can slide under the door.

Patient: Are you sure I'm suffering from pneumonia? I heard about a doctor treating someone for pneumonia and the patient died from tuberculosis.
Doctor: Don't worry. That won't happen with me. If I treat a patient for pneumonia, he will die from pneumonia.

Doctor: I can't find a cause for your complaint. Frankly, I think it's alcohol.
Patient: In that case, I'll come back when you're sober.

The patient rattled off a laundry list of the diseases he thought he was suffering from.
Doctor: The trouble with you is you're a hypochondriac.
Patient: Oh, no! Don't tell me I've got that as well.

Patient: Doc, I think I'm getting senile. Several times lately, I have forgotten to zip up.
Doctor: That's not senility. Senility is when you forget to zip down.

Patient: Doc, I have sex about six times a year.
Doctor: That's not much.
Patient: That's not too bad for a priest without a car.

GOOD NEWS-BAD NEWS

Doctor: I'm afraid you're dying.
Patient: How long do I have?

Doctor: Ten.
Patient: Ten what? Ten months, ten weeks, ten minutes?
Doctor: Ten, nine, eight, seven . . .

Doctor: My examination indicates you have only six months to live.
    You should get married so there will be someone to look after you
    during the final stages. I suggest you marry a Jewish girl.
Patient: Why a Jewish girl?
Doctor: Because the time will seem longer.

A man, who constantly gasped for breath, causing his eyes to bulge
    was given a month to live by his doctor. He decided to go on a
    shopping spree.
Man: I want two dozen of those very expensive shirts, size 14.
Clerk: You're neck looks bigger than a 14. You need a 16.
Man: I know my size. I want all those shirts in a 14.
Clerk: Okay, but I want to warn you. If you wear a 14, you'll gasp for
    air all day and your eyes will bulge.

Doctor: I've got good new and bad news.
Patient: What's the bad news?
Doctor: You only have three more minutes of life.
Patient: So, what's the good news?
Doctor: They're going to name the disease after you.

Doctor: I have good news and bad news.
Patient: Lay it one me, doc. What's the bad news?
Doctor: You have Alzheimer's disease.
Patient: What's the good news?
Doctor: You can go home and forget about it.

Emergency room doctor: Hello? Your wife was in a terrible automobile
    accident. We have bad news and good news. The bad news is that
    we had to amputate her arms and her feet. She will need your
    help eating and going to the bathroom for the rest of her life.
Husband: My God! What's the good news?
Doctor: We're kidding. She's dead.

ALWAYS MONEY

Doctor on the phone: Your check came back!
Patient: So did my bursitis.

The patient was concerned about the enormous price the doctor was
  charging for the operation.
Doctor: Can you pay $460.75 a month?
Patient: I can do that, but it sounds like a funny amount. It sounds like
  you're buying a car.
Doctor: I am.

Doctor to patient: I believe you will need an operation.
Patient: Doc, I don't have money or medical insurance. Is there
  anything you can do?
Doctor, thinking: Well, I can touch up these x-rays.

Hospital administrator: Why are you so worried?
Patient: Will my operation be dangerous?
Administrator: No, you can't get a dangerous operation for five
  hundred dollars.

Patient: How much for the penile transplant.
Doctor: It will cost twenty-five thousand dollars, but then again, it
  will bring back your sex life. Why don't you go home and talk it
  over with your wife. Call me in the morning with your decision.
Patient: Good morning, doc. We talked it over and we decided to
  redo the kitchen instead.

SURGEONS, A CUT ABOVE THE REST

Surgeon to Patient: This is Nurse Smith. She has a very bad case of
  halitosis and will be French kissing you during your operation.
Patient: Why?
Surgeon: Because we are running out of anesthesia.

Nurse in operating room: What are we operating for?
Surgeon: Five thousand dollars.
Nurse: You don't understand. I mean, what does he have?
Surgeon: I told you, five thousand dollars.

Young lady to surgeon: Doc, how long will I have to wait to have sex after my operation?
Surgeon: You're the first person to ever ask that question before a tonsillectomy.

Young lady to surgeon: Do you think the scar will show after my bust enlargement operation?
Surgeon: That's entirely up to you,

Hospital administrator to patient: Why did you run out of the operating room this morning?
Patient: Because the nurse said, "Get hold of yourself and don't be so jittery. An appendectomy is a very simple operation."
Administrator: So?
Patient: So! She was talking to the surgeon.

Surgeon to Nurse: Oh, I can't believe it. My patient just expired.
Nurse, weeping loudly: My what a shock! It's horrible, simply awful.
Surgeon: Lighten up. It's not as though we're making a movie.

PSYCHIATRISTS ARE SHRINKS, TOO

Patient: Doc, you gotta help me. I'm under a lot of pressure. I keep losing my temper with people.
Psychiatrist: Tell me your problem.
Patient: I just did, you fuckin' ass hole!

Couple to Psychiatrist: You gave us good advice to improve our sex life. You told us to act immediately when we felt like making love. Last night, at dinner, we reached for the salt as the same time, and our fingers touched. We were ecstatic. We swept the salt away and made love right there and then on the table. It was glorious. But, of course, we can never go back to Denny's again.

Agitated young man to psychiatrist: I dreamt I saw my mother in the kitchen last night. She turned around and had your face. I couldn't go back to sleep. I got out of bed, drank a coke and rushed right over here. Please, tell me why I would have this dream.
Psychiatrist: A coke! A coke! You call that breakfast.

Young girl to psychiatrist: I'm still hazy about the phallus symbol. What is a phallus symbol, again?
Psychiatrist unzips his pants to better explain: Now this here thing, young lady, is a phallus.
Young girl: Oh, I see. You mean it's like a prick, but only smaller.

Patient: Doctor, I sleep walk every night and wake up in the kitchen.
Shrink: So, would you like me to cure the sleepwalking?
Patient: That's not exactly the problem. Every time I wake up in the kitchen I have my penis in the peanut jar.
Shrink: I think I know what your problem is. You're fuckin' nuts.

Patient: I suffer from premature ejaculation. Can you help me?
Shrink: No, but I can introduce you to a woman with a short attention span.

Shrink: If you want to cure your insomnia, you must stop taking your troubles to bed with you.
Patient: I know, but I can't. My wife refuses to sleep alone.

Shrink to married couple: First, let's find some common ground. Tell me about anything you two have in common?
Husband: Neither one of us sucks dicks. That's it.
Shrink: You really don't have very much in common. Why on earth did you get married?

Wife: I suppose it was the old business of opposites attract. He wasn't pregnant and I was.

Shrink: For the past year we have gone through word association, dream analysis, delved into the faithful subconscious, and explored many other possibilities. I can now tell you the good news.
Patient: Thanks, doc. Does this mean I no longer have an inferiority complex?
Shrink: No, and you never did. You really are inferior.

Man to friend: I just quit seeing my psychiatrist. He listened to me for five years, two, sometimes three times a week, nodded and set the next appointment.
Friend: Did he ever say anything to you.
Man: Yes, just yesterday.
Friend: What did he say?
Man: No hablo Ingles.

Patient to psychiatrist: I've been talking to myself.
Psychiatrist: Don't worry. Many people do the same thing.
Patient: Yes, but you don't know what a pain in the ass I can be.

Patient: Doctor, my wife is being unfaithful. Every night she goes to the same bar and picks up some guy. She'll sleep with anyone who asks her. I'm going crazy with worry. What should I do?
Psychiatrist: Just relax. Take a couple of deep breaths and try to calm down. Now, first of all, tell me exactly where this bar is.

Patient: I've got that old song, DELILAH, running through my head every minute of the day. I can't shake it and it's driving me nuts.
Psychiatrist: Sounds like the Tom Jones Syndrome to me.
Patient: Is it a rare disorder?
Psychiatrist: "It's not unusual".

OPTOMETRISTS ARE EYE DOCTORS, TOO

Receptionist: What's the problem?
Patient: I keep seeing spots in front of my eyes.
Receptionist: Have you seen an eye doctor before?
Patient: No, just spots.

Patient opens door in the optometrist's office: Hello? I think I need my eyes checked.
Woman sitting on the can: You're not kidding, mister. This is the ladies room.

AUDIOLOGISTS SHOULD HEAR THIS

Man to ear doctor: How much do hearing aids cost?
Doctor: It depends upon the model. They start at five dollars and go up to five thousand dollars.
Man: Show me the five dollar model?
Doctor: Just stick this ear piece in your ear and run the length of the wire into your pocket.
Man: Will this really work?
Doctor: In all honesty, no. But, when people see it on you they will talk louder.

DENTISTS ARE DOCTORS, TOO

Patient: How much does it cost to have a tooth pulled?
Dentist: $125.00
Patient: So much for just a few minutes of work?
Dentist: I can extract it very slowly if you like.

Kid to dentist: Look, I want a tooth taken out fast. No gas, no Novocain, no nuttin', 'cause I'm in a hurry.
Dentist: I must say you're a very brave little boy. Which tooth is it?

Kid to friend: Show him your tooth, Albert.

Dentist: You need an enormous amount of dental work done.
Patient: I was afraid of that. Believe me, I'd rather have a baby.
Dentist: Make up your mind, before I finish adjusting the chair.

She was pretty and married and lured into passionate daily encounters
   with her dentist
Dentist: We've got to stop seeing each other. Your husband is bound
   to get suspicious of all these dental visits.
She: No way. He's as dumb as a post. He doesn't suspect a thing.
Dentist: True, but you're down to one tooth.

PHARMACISTS

MEDICS, DOCTORS, DENTISTS, PSYCHIATRISTS,
ALL ROLLED INTO ONE

Woman to pharmacist: I need some arsenic, please
Pharmacist: What may I ask do you need the arsenic for?
Woman: I want to kill my husband.
Pharmacist: I can't sell you any for such a use.
Woman: Look, here. See this photo of a man and a woman clearly
   having sex. Well, the man is my husband, and I'm sure you
   recognized your wife.
Pharmacist: Oh, I didn't know you had a prescription. I'll get the
   arsenic immediately.

The man rushes into the drug store and seeks out the pharmacist.
Man: Can you stop hiccups right away?
Without warning, the pharmacist slaps him twice across his face.
Man: What was that for?
Pharmacist: Well, you don't have hiccups anymore, do you?
Man: No, but my wife, sitting in the car, still does.

Customer to pharmacist: Can you tell me where I can find Dr.
    Johnson's medicated talcum powder?
Pharmacist: If you walk this way, madam, I'll show you where it is.
Customer: Oy. If I could walk that way, would I need it?

Out of curiosity, I asked my brother, Kenny, who was once a
druggist, but is now a pharmacist, what doctors actually scribbled
on their prescriptions. "That's easy," he said, as he showed me an
example that read, "I've got my fifty bucks, now get yours!"

CHAPTER THIRTY-ONE

LAWYERS AND THE BIBLE

THE WORD, "LAWYER," is never mentioned in the Old Testament. However, the word, "lawyer," is mentioned in the Gospel of Luke. Certain Jewish leaders, officials within various communities, were portrayed as hostel to Jesus. The Greek term for lawyer is found only once in the Gospel of Matthew with an uncertain explanation. Luke seems to define these people better. "They have been accused of asking questions that provoke Jesus' teachings and condone parables illustrating the nature of the Kingdom of God." So, given this damning ancient view, we ask, so what else is new? We do know that having lawyers make laws is like having doctors make diseases.

Teacher: Now class, please tell us what your father does for a living.

Billy: My daddy plays the piano in a whorehouse.

Teacher, on the phone with Billy's father: Why would you tell a young child a thing like that?

Father: Actually, I'm a lawyer, but how do you explain that to a seven year old.

Lawyer to electrician: Why are you charging ninety dollars an hour for repairs? I don't make that much as a lawyer.
Electrician: I didn't either when I was a lawyer.

Lawyer: St. Peter, I was only thirty-five years old at the time of the accident. How could you have done this to me?
St. Peter: Wow! When we looked at your hourly billings we thought you were about ninety.

Man: Are you a lawyer?
Lawyer: Yes.
Man: How much do you charge?
Lawyer: A hundred dollars for four questions.
Man: Isn't that awfully expensive?
Lawyer: Yes. And what's your fourth question?

Client: I don't understand your five hundred dollar charge for luncheon advice.
Lawyer: Don't you remember? I advised you to order the chicken breast with potato slices instead of rice.

Lawyer calls Governor: Judge Smith just died and I want to take his place.
Governor: Well, it's okay with me if it's okay with the mortuary.

Woman: I need your help to get a divorce.
Lawyer: On what grounds?
Woman: My husband's getting a little queer to sleep with.
Lawyer: Does he force you to indulge in unusual sex practices?
Woman: No, neither does the little queer.

Judge: I have reviewed this case very carefully. Given the facts, I've decided to give your wife six hundred dollars a month. You may comment if you wish.
Lawyer, whispering to his client: Tell the judge you thinks that's fair, and every now and then you'll kick in a few bucks to her as well.

The Mafia was enraged that a Mexican hired hand had absconded with the loot stolen in a bank heist. They sent an enforcer to Mexico City to recover the money. The Mafia's Spanish speaking lawyer accompanied him. The traitor was tracked down and accosted. The enforcer asked the lawyer to find out where the money was hidden.

Lawyer: He told me to go to Hell.

Enforcer: Ask him again.

Lawyer: He said you should screw yourself.

The enforcer is so enraged, he shoots the hired hand in the leg: Tell him the next shot will go between his eyes.

Hired hand, coming to his senses yells out in Spanish: Okay, okay. Tell him the money is in the trunk of my car under the spare tire.

Lawyer: He says he's not afraid to die.

A lawyer opens the door of his BMW automobile. A speeding car hits the door and rips it off.

Lawyer: Officer, look what they did to my car.

Policeman: You lawyers are so materialistic. You make me sick. You're so worried about your stupid car, you haven't noticed your left arm was ripped off.

Lawyer: Oh, my God. Where's my Rolex?

A man was standing in line waiting to purchase a movie theatre ticket when suddenly he felt the guy behind him massaging his shoulders.

Man: Hey? What the hell are you doing?

Other man, stammering: Oh, I'm terribly sorry. I'm a chiropractor and I could see you were pretty tense. Out of habit, I started to rub your shoulders to release the tension and help you relax.

Man: That's a bunch of shit, buddy. I'm a lawyer, and you don't see me screwing the guy in front of me.

CHAPTER THIRTY-TWO

ART AND THE BIBLE

STORIES FROM THE Bible inspired early artists to use important events as subjects of narrative art. The Bible influenced mosaics in churches throughout the Christian world. Many of the frescos were interpretations of Biblical stories that related powerful religious meaning. Relief sculptures used human characters from the Old and the New Testaments. The unifying theme was often salvation through Christ. The Bible influenced artists through the Renaissance era. Art changed from flat two-dimensional paintings to more realistic three-dimensional works.

Rembrandt is considered one of the great commentators of the Bible. Marc Chagall's paintings, etchings, and stained glass works constitute a uniquely important interpretation of the Bible.

Two statues, one male and one female, had religiously guarded the door to an old church for five centuries. One day, God in his mercy, decided to give them a day off.

God: Spend the day anyway you want.

Male: We are going into the bushes.

After twelve hours of rattling and shaking in a frenzy of activity, the pair emerged.

God: You've still got half a day left. Go off and have some more fun.

Female to male: Okay. This time you hold the pigeons down, and I'll crap all over them.

Woman in Art Gallery to Artist: I'm sorry, but I don't understand your paintings. This one is just bright blue with orange swirls in all directions, and the other is a mess of small black and lime green blobs.

Artist: I paint what I feel inside of me.

Woman: Have you tried Alka-Seltzer?

Woman in Museum: I suppose you call this hideous looking piece an example of modern art?

Tour guide: No, Madam. That one is called a mirror.

CHAPTER THIRTY-THREE

TRAVEL AND THE BIBLE

TO TRAVEL IN Ancient Times usually meant to walk. As people and animals traversed the same paths over and over again, they created roads in the dirt. By King Solomon's era, horses and chariots, formerly used exclusively for warfare, were now used for travel. The Romans improved the roads throughout their empire during the period of the New Testament. When Jesus was born the seventy-five mile trip from Nazareth to Bethlehem took five days to complete. The trip Mary, Joseph and Jesus took to Egypt was more than two hundred miles each way. They walked most of the way even though they probably had a donkey. There were many sailing ships carrying goods and occasional passengers. Travel was not easy or pleasant. Often, modern travel is not pleasant either.

An airliner experienced an unusually bumpy landing. After they taxied to the terminal, the sheepish pilot took his station at the exit door, thanking the passengers. He braced himself to grin and bear obvious comments. However, everyone exited nodding very politely, except for the last passenger. A little old lady with a cane came forward.

Little old lady: Captain, mind if I ask you a question?

Captain: Why, no, not at all. What is it?

Little old lady: Captain, were we shot down?

Female passenger, stripping naked as the plane heads for a crash landing. If I'm going to die, I want to die feeling like a woman.

Male passenger, removing his pants: Here! Iron these!

IRS man to Deli owner: We want to know about the $100,000 profit you reported.

Deli owner: We work like maniacs all year. My wife works with me seven days a week from morning to night.

IRS man: It's not your income that troubles us, it's the $80,000 business travel deduction. You and your wife made ten trips to Israel.

Deli owner: Oh, My God! I forgot to report, we deliver.

The turbulence finally got to the little old Jewish man. He vomited all over a rough husky Texan sleeping next to him.

Old man, nudging and awakening the Texan: Do you feel better now?

After an hour of turbulence, the captain put the plane on automatic pilot, tilted his chair back, took a deep breath and laid back to relax.

Captain: What I need now is a hot cup of coffee and a good blow job.

The captain was unaware that the speakers were on throughout the aircraft and everyone could hear him. A stewardees bolted out of her seat racing down the aisle to shut down the speaker system.

Little old man, yelling loudly as she flew down the aisle: And don't' forget, miss, he also wants hot coffee.

CHAPTER THIRTY-FOUR

SPORTS AND THE BIBLE

S PORTS AND GAMES are rarely mentioned in the Bible. Archaeologists have dug up some board games from the time of the Old Testament. Chess might have been played in Israel. Old carvings suggest boys played tug-of-war and girls juggled balls. The New Testament refers to Greek foot races, chariot races, discus and javelin throwing, horse racing and bow and arrow sporting events. The apostle Paul may have watched wrestling matches in his travels. He used a picture of a wrestling position to describe how Christians must struggle against Satan. The most famous painting in the Bible depicts Jacob and God's Angel wrestling.

CHRISTIAN VALUES AND SPORTS

Coach to church baseball team: Hopefully, you kids will grow up to be good Christians. Do you know what cooperation and sportsmanship are?
Team, in unison: Yes, coach.

Coach: When a strike is called, or if you're caught stealing a base, don't argue or attack the umpire. Do you understand?

Team, in unison: Yes, coach.

Coach: And, when I pull you out of the game for no reason, you do not argue, curse or attack me. Do you understand?

Team, in unison: Yes, coach.

Coach: Now, go and explain all this to your mothers and fathers.

BASEBALL FOR DUMMIES

Wife at a ballgame: Why does the man behind the batter wear an iron mask and such a big baby bib? He looks so silly,

Husband: It's to keep the catcher's shirt clean from getting spattered with blood, in case a ball happens to knock his teeth out.

Catcher to Rookie Pitcher: I've figured out your problem. You lose control at the same point every game.

Pitcher: When is that?

Catcher: Right after the National Anthem.

Little Billy: Dad, you won't believe this, but I was responsible for the winning run.

Dad: How'd you do it?

Little Billy: I dropped the ball.

Manager at mound: I think you've had enough.

Pitcher: But, I struck this guy out the last time he was up.

Manager: I know, but this is the same inning.

COUCH POTATOES

Wife: I've become a football widow. My husband is glued to the TV set and doesn't pay any attention to me.

Friend: Wear something sheer during the game,

Wife: What if that doesn't work?
Friend: Then put a number on your back.

Wife, closing TV set: I'm disgusted seeing you watch sports on TV all the time. Sports, sports, sports, that's all there is. You haven't touched me in over a month. I must insist we talk about sex.
Husband: Sure, I'll start. How often do you think A-rod gets laid every week?

Wife, day one: Honey, the toilet is broken.
Husband: Who do I look like, a plumber? I'm watching football.
Wife, day two: Honey, the vacuum cleaner is not working.
Husband: Who do I look like, Mr. Hoover? I'm watching a baseball game.
Wife, day three: Honey, the washing machine is out of order.
Husband: Who do I look like, the Maytag man? I'm watching a basketball game.
Wife, day four: Honey, I had all the repairmen in the house today.
Husband: How much is this all going to cost?
Wife: Well, honey, they all said I could pay them either by baking a cake or having sex with them.
Husband: What kind of cakes did you bake for them?
Wife: Who do I look like, Betty Crocker?

GOLF FANATICS

Woman, hacking away at golf balls: I guess all those fuckin' lessons I took over the winter didn't help.
Male golfer, watching: Now I see your problem. You should have taken golf lessons instead.

Novice, taking lessons from a famous golf pro: You are spectacular. Your name is synonymous with the game of golf. You really know your way around the course. What's your secret?
Golf Pro: The holes are numbered.

Golfer #1: I understand you experienced a great tragedy last week.

Golfer #2: You're right. I was playing with Joe and the poor fellow dropped dead at the ninth hole.

Golfer #1: They tell me you carried him back to the clubhouse. That must have been very difficult. He weighed 200 pounds.

Golfer #2: It wasn't the carrying that was hard. It was putting him down with every stroke I took and then picking him up.

The bride reaches the altar and whispers to the groom: What are your golf clubs doing here?

Groom: This isn't going to take all day, is it?

Man, at golf clubhouse, takes a cell phone call:

Woman: Honey, it's me. I'm on the speaker phone.

Man: Yes?

Woman: I'm at the mall. I found a beautiful leather coat marked down from $7,000 to $4,500. Can I buy it?

Man: Go ahead, if you like it that much.

Woman: Thanks. I also stopped by the Mercedes dealership and looked at the new models. I saw a red one. I really love it.

Man: How much was it?

Woman: $70,000.

Man: For that price I want all the options.

Woman: Great, I'm sure I can get that. One more thing: the house we wanted is back on the market. They're asking $3,500,000 for it now.

Man: Okay, go ahead and buy the sucker, but don't offer more than $3,400,000.

Woman: That will work. See you later.

The other golfers heard his conversation and looked at him in amazement.

Man, shouts out: Does anyone know who owns this cell phone?

The golfer was lining up a putt. If successful, he would earn the ten thousand dollar prize. He stopped when a funeral procession passed, took his hat off and placed it against his heart.

Buddy: I can't believe you stopped playing, possibly losing your concentration, to pay your respects.

Golfer: Well, we WERE married twenty-five years.

JUST PLAIN BULL

Tour guide at a bullfight in a South American country: This is our number one sport.

Tourist: Isn't it revolting?

Tour guide: No, that's our number two sport.

GETTING BACK TO ISRAEL

A worker was renovating an old building in Jerusalem. He fell through the roof into an undiscovered cellar. After the dust settled, he noticed a skeleton on the ground with an Israeli banner draped across the chest. It read, "All-Israeli Hide and Seek Champion, 1948."

The Tel-Aviv University rowing team practiced for hours daily, but lost race after race. They decided to send their captain to Cambridge to spy on their daily practices.

Captain, upon returning: Guys, I figured out their secret.

Team, in unison: Tell us! How? Who? When? Where? What?

Captain: We should only have one guy yelling. The other eight should row.

Olympic announcer: .38.3 seconds; France wins gold. 37.7 seconds; Germany wins silver. 36.0 seconds; Italy wins bronze.

Israeli coach to Israeli skier: What happened? You beat all those guys easily in the trials.

Skier: Who the fuck put a mezuzah on every gate?

POSTCRIPT

LET'S GET SERIOUS NOW

THE FUTURE OF MAN AND LIFE
AND THE NEW EVOLUTION

EVOLUTION IS STILL happening today and will continue for many millions of years. With our present knowledge and education, it would be futile to predict the changes of the future, but human beings already have the ability to control evolution.

Some theorize evolution is finished; life has completed evolving. They argue that evolution had a single goal, the appearance of man. An intelligent being alive during the Jurassic period might have believed the same. Existing life must have appeared complete without future opportunities.

At this point in time we have to consider possibilities. What happens if man is wiped out by a single catastrophic event? It is improbable that anything similar to man would redevelop. However, it is true that human-like intelligence, individual responsibility and adaptability have selective value in evolution, and another animal could develop such traits. It is safe to predict that no other mammal will compete with man and his unique human characteristics as long as man does exist. Man has a firm grip on his place on Earth and is fully able to defend it.

The New Evolution is the accumulation of new knowledge and the rise of new values. New human social evolution depends upon expanded learning. It is unwise to believe mankind is already intelligent enough for its own good. The most brilliant persons do not have enough learning capacity to acquire all the details of every field of knowledge outside their specialty. The New Evolution demands a larger brain. The additional educational needs during the critical early years will have to be met.

While the most essential factor in the New Evolution is the expansion of knowledge by way of greater brainpower, value judgments coupled with the highest moral ethical standards are likewise necessary. Knowledge will be acquired and desirable for the future when strong ethical codes are in place. The primary goal will be avoiding at all costs self-extinction by settling ideological battles and progressing toward an ethically good world state.

The New Evolutionary Man broadly manipulates the environment and is learning how to do so more and more. He knows evolution occurs and is learning exactly how it works. This makes it possible for him to guide his own changes and those of any other organisms he chooses. Man is rapidly learning to control life and death. He has already caused the extinction of numerous species and is capable of devising means for selective extinction at will.

Man is quite capable of wiping himself out without a catastrophic event in the future. If his extinction is long delayed it is reasonably certain he will further evolve and change radically. Space travel is another option for the survival of Man. Thus, no matter what transpires on planet Earth, the New Evolution of Man may be altered, but never stopped.

Astronomer Carl Sagan explored the likelihood there were advanced civilizations that could exist in our own galaxy or universe. "When one considers the fact that there are billions of galaxies with billions of stars, with some galaxies containing stars numbering thousands more times than our galaxy, the prospect for other intelligent life is more of a possibility. Actually it is more realistic to believe that life in other worlds is no longer a probability."

Astronomer Timothy Ferris, a National Geographic contributor, ponders the possibilities of seeking new earths. "It took humans thousands of years to explore our own planet and centuries to comprehend our neighboring planets, but nowadays new worlds are being discovered every week. Astronomers have discovered nearly four hundred planet worlds orbiting stars other than our sun. However, no planets quite like ours have yet to be found, because they're inconspicuous. To see a planet as small and dim as Earth amid the glare of its 'sun' is like trying to see a firefly in a fireworks display. To detect its gravitational influence on its 'sun' is like listening for a cricket in a tornado. Yet, by pushing technology to the limits, astronomers are rapidly approaching the day when they can find another Earth and search it for signs of some sort of life. In the search for extraterrestrial life scientists are well aware that it may be different from life at home. Life thrived on Earth for billions of years before land plants appeared and populated the continents. The curtain is going up on countless new worlds like or unlike ours. In any event, be it on Earth or outer space, Man will not merely endure, he will prevail. He is immortal, not because he alone among creatures has an inexhaustible voice, but because he has a soul, a spirit capable of compassion and sacrifice and endurance."

I personally experienced the truism that Biblical Creation and evolution does indeed co-exist today, especially with the younger generations. On two recent visits to the Galapagos Islands where Charles Darwin finally and definitively established evolution as a fact, I encountered numerous young naturalists, biologists, geologists and the like. They were mostly Roman Catholics from various parts of South America. Many wore the cross of Jesus and various religious medals and were teaching evolution to visitors with great conviction and enthusiasm.

Obviously, they did not dismiss their religious beliefs or were they apt to repeat the mistake of denial of their elders or ancestors either. How could they do this, one might ask? Yes, they believed in the evolutionary process. Whether God was or was not responsible is not an issue. They view God as an inspirational and morally guiding force necessary for man today. Perhaps the concept of God, as taught, will not survive in Man's New Evolution. This was not an issue for them either.

There are early signs that the New Evolution of Man is beginning to quicken its pace. Yet, in evolutionary terms, it's just a wink. Never-the-less one can detect that wink. Those of us who are approaching octogenarian age will attest by observation that today's children are by far more intelligent, brighter, inquisitive and worldly than we were. Evolution has moved at a snails pace in the past, but it seems to have gotten a nudge. Now, it seems to take less than a hundred years to participate in Man's New Evolution. There is no doubt knowledge and truth are the chief ingredients. We will be able to have a clearer understanding of the lives we lead and a more positive and healthy outlook only by consistently trying to seek the truth. If we can begin to measure movement towards the New Evolution by a century, we can never contemplate Man's place in nature hundreds, thousands or even millions of years from now.

THE NEW MESSIAH

Messiah is the Hebrew word for the anointed one. The term denotes an expected or long awaited savior. The Jewish people are expecting a political leader. In contrast, the disciples realized Jesus Christ was the spiritual savior sent by God who would give new meaning to life on earth through all eternity. Jesus himself taught that he was the Messiah. Thus, the Jewish Messiah saves people from danger and the Christian messiah saves people from sin. Both groups believe that those loving God will live together in a fellowship forever and ever.

The confrontation between scientific evolution and religion is a natural consequence of Man's search for the truth. It defends his place in this universe. The scientific approach is based on facts, which allow Man to use deductive logic and reasoning powers to control his external world. The religious approach is based upon spiritual revelations that tell Man how to conduct a moral life in conformance with his God's commands.

The New Evolution is on track to produce a new Messiah – a Messiah, not in the image of man, but a Messiah of truth and knowledge, having the same Judaic-Christian values and expectations.

A group of eminent scientists decided Man had come a long way and no longer needed God.

Spokesman to God: We can clone people and do many wondrous things. We really don't need you anymore and we think you should retire.

God: Okay, but first let us both make a man just like I did with Adam. Then, we can compare our work.

Spokesman, as he bends down to scoop up a handful of dirt: Let's do that.

God: Oh no you don't! Go get your own dirt.

Now, it's time for the reader to ask me what I personally believe. I offer a poem I have titled:

TORN AND TROUBLED

I believe in the sun, even if it's not shining.

I believe in love, even when I'm not feeling it.

I believe in God, even when He is silent.

I believe God has a sense of humor, even if I can't hear Him laughing.

And I believe, perhaps, Man's New Evolution is coming without our Lord.

(BUT GOD, I SAID, "PERHAPS.")

Edwards Brothers,Inc!
Thorofare, NJ 08086
27 September, 2010
BA2010270